THE ARABS IN HISTORY

the text of this book is printed
on 100% recycled paper

THE *ARABS* IN HISTORY

Bernard Lewis
Professor of the History of the Near and Middle East in the University of London

HARPER COLOPHON BOOKS
Harper & Row, Publishers
New York, Hagerstown, San Francisco, London

THE ARABS IN HISTORY

This book was first published in 1950 in the History division (edited by Joel Hurstfield) of the Hutchinson University Library, with 2nd, 3rd and 4th revised editions published in 1958, 1964, and 1966, respectively. It is here reprinted by arrangement with Hutchinson & Co., Ltd., London.

The first Harper Torchbook edition was published in 1960. The second Harper Torchbook edition was published in 1967 by Harper & Row, Publishers, Incorporated, 10 East 53rd Street, New York, N.Y. 10022.

ISBN: 0-06-090491-7

79 80 20

CONTENTS

PREFACE

THIS is not so much a history of the Arabs as an essay in interpretation. Rather than compress so vast a subject into a bare outline of dates and events, I have sought to isolate and examine certain basic issues—the place of the Arabs in human history, their identity, their achievement, and the salient characteristics of the several ages of their development.

In a work of this nature it is not possible nor indeed desirable to acknowledge the sources of every point of fact and interpretation. Orientalists will recognise at once my debt to the masters, past and present, of Islamic historical studies. For the rest, I can only express my general indebtedness to my predecessors, teachers, colleagues and students who have all helped, in different ways, to form the view of Arab history set forth in these pages.

My special thanks are due to Professor Sir Hamilton Gibb, Professor U. Heyd, and the late Professor D. S. Rice for reading and criticising my manuscript, to Miss J. Bridges for preparing the Index, and to Professor A. T. Hatto for many useful suggestions.

B.L.

INTRODUCTION

WHAT is an Arab? Ethnic terms are notoriously difficult to define, and Arab is not among the easiest. One possible definition may be set aside at once. The Arabs may be a nation; they are not as yet a nationality in the legal sense. A man who calls himself an Arab may be described in his passport as of Iraqi or Jordanian, Syrian or Lebanese, Yemeni or Sa'ūdī Arabian, Libyan or Sudanese, Tunisian, Algerian, or Moroccan nationality. If he is from Egypt, he may be described as a citizen of the United Arab Republic, the name adopted at the time of the Syro-Egyptian union in 1958, and retained by Egypt after its dissolution. He will not, however, be simply described as an Arab. There are Arab states, and indeed a league of Arab states; but as yet there is no single Arab state of which all Arabs are nationals.

But if Arabism has no legal content, it is none the less real. The pride of the Arab in his Arabdom, his consciousness of the bonds that bind him to other Arabs past and present, are no less intense. Is the unifying factor then one of language—is an Arab simply one who speaks Arabic as his mother tongue? It is a simple and at first sight a satisfying answer—yet there are difficulties. Is the Arabic-speaking Jew of Iraq or the Yemen or the Arabic-speaking Christian of Egypt or Lebanon an Arab? The enquirer could receive different answers amongst these people themselves and among their Muslim neighbours. Is even the Arabic-speaking Muslim of Egypt an Arab? Many consider themselves such, but not all, and the term Arab is still used colloquially in both Egypt and Iraq to distinguish the Bedouin of the surrounding deserts from the indigenous peasantry of the great river valleys. In some quarters the repellent word Arabophone is used to distinguish those who merely speak Arabic from those who are truly Arabs.

A gathering of Arab leaders some years ago defined an Arab in these words: "Whoever lives in our country, speaks our language, is brought up in our culture and takes pride in our glory is one of us." We may compare with this a definition from a well-qualified Western source, Professor Gibb of Harvard: "All those are Arabs for whom the central fact of history is the mission of Muhammad and the memory of the Arab Empire and who in addition cherish the Arabic tongue and its cultural heritage as their common possession." Neither definition, it will be noted, is purely linguistic. Both add a cultural, one at least a religious, qualification. Both must be interpreted historically, for it is only through the history of the peoples called Arab that we can hope to understand the meaning of the term from its primitive restricted use in ancient times to its vast but vaguely delimited extent of meaning today. As we shall see, through this long period the significance of the word Arab has been steadily changing, and as the change has been slow, complex and extensive, we shall find that the term may be used in several different senses at one and the same time and that a standard general definition of its content has rarely been possible.

The origin of the word Arab is still obscure, though philologists have offered explanations of varying plausibility. For some, the word is derived from a Semitic root meaning "west", and was first applied by the inhabitants of Mesopotamia to the peoples to the west of the Euphrates valley. This etymology is questionable on purely linguistic grounds and is also open to the objection that the term was used by the Arabs themselves and that a people is not likely to describe itself by a word indicating its position relative to another. More profitable are the attempts to link the word with the concept of nomadism. This has been done in various ways; by connecting it with the Hebrew "*'Arābhā*"—dark land, or steppe land; with the Hebrew "*'Erebh*"—mixed and hence unorganised, as opposed to the organised and ordered life of the sedentary communities, rejected and despised by the nomads; with the root "*'Ābhar*"—to move or pass—from which our word Hebrew is probably derived. The association with nomadism is borne out by the fact that the Arabs themselves seem to have used the word at an early date to distinguish the Bedouin from the Arabic-speaking town and village dwellers and indeed continue to do so to some extent at the present day. The traditional Arab etymology deriving the name from a verb meaning "to express" or "enunciate" is almost certainly a reversal of the historic process. A parallel case may be found in the connexion between German "deuten"—"to make clear to the people", and "deutsch"—originally "of the people".

The earliest account that has come down to us of Arabia and the Arabs is that of the tenth chapter of Genesis, where many of the peoples and districts of the peninsula are mentioned by name. The word Arab, however, does not occur in this text, and makes its first appearance in an Assyrian inscription of 853 B.C. in which King Shalmaneser III records the defeat by the Assyrian forces of a conspiracy of rebellious princelings; one of them was "Gindibu the Aribi" who appropriately contributed 1,000 camels to the forces of the confederacy. From that time until the sixth century B.C. there are frequent references in Assyrian and Babylonian inscriptions to Aribi, Arabu, and Urbi. These inscriptions record the receipt of tribute from Aribi rulers, usually including camels and other items indicative of a desert origin, and occasionally tell of military expeditions into Aribi land. Some of the later inscriptions are accompanied by illustrations of the Aribi and their camels. These campaigns against the Aribi were clearly not wars of conquest but punitive expeditions intended to recall the erring nomads to their duties as Assyrian vassels. They served the general purpose of securing the Assyrian borderlands and lines of communication. The Aribi of the inscriptions are a nomadic people living in the far north of Arabia, probably in the Syro-Arabian desert. They do not include the flourishing sedentary civilisation of south-western Arabia which is separately mentioned in Assyrian records. They may be identified with the Arabs of the later books of the Old Testament. Towards 530 B.C. the term Arabaya begins to appear in Persian cuneiform documents.

The earliest classical reference is in Aeschylus, who in "Prometheus" mentions Arabia as a remote land whence come warriors with sharp-pointed spears. The "*Magos Arabos*" mentioned in the "Persians" as one of the commanders of Xerxes' army may possibly also be an Arab. It is in Greek writings that we find for the first time the place-name Arabia, formed on the analogy of Italia, etc. Herodotus and after him most other Greek and Latin writers extend the terms Arabia and Arab to the entire peninsula and all its inhabitants including the southern Arabians, and even the eastern desert of Egypt between the Nile and the Red Sea. The term at this time thus seems to cover all the desert areas of the Near and Middle East inhabited by semitic-speaking peoples. It is in Greek literature, too, that the term "Saracen" first becomes common. This word first appears in the ancient inscriptions and seems to be the name of a single desert tribe in the Sinai area. In Greek, Latin and Talmudic literature it is used of the nomads generally, and in Byzantium and the mediaeval West was later applied to all Muslim peoples.

The first Arabian use of the word Arab occurs in the ancient southern Arabian inscriptions, those relics of the flourishing civilisation set up in the Yemen by the southern branch of the Arab peoples and dating from the late pre-Christian and early Christian centuries. In these, Arab means Bedouin, often raider, and is applied to the nomadic as distinct from the sedentary population. The first occurrence in the north is in the early fourth-century A.D. Namāra Epitaph, one of the oldest surviving records in the north-Arabian language which later became classical Arabic. This inscription, written in Arabic but in the Nabatean Aramaic script, records the death and achievements of Imru'l-Qais, "King of all the Arabs", in terms which suggest that the sovereignty claimed did not extend far beyond the nomads of northern and central Arabia.

It is not until the rise of Islam early in the seventh century that we have any real information as to the use of the word in central and northern Arabia. For Muḥammad and his contemporaries the Arabs were the Bedouin of the desert, and in the Qur'ān the term is used exclusively in this sense and never of the townsfolk of Mecca, Medina and other cities. On the other hand, the language of these towns and of the Qur'ān itself is described as Arabic. Here we find already the germ of the idea prevalent in later times that the purest form of Arabic is that of the Bedouin, who have preserved more faithfully than any others the original Arab way of life and speech.

The great waves of conquest that followed the death of Muḥammad and the establishment of the Caliphate by his successors in the headship of the new Islamic community wrote the name Arab large across the three continents of Asia, Africa and Europe, and placed it in the heading of a vital though not lengthy chapter in the history of human thought and endeavour. The Arabic-speaking peoples of Arabia, nomad and settled folk alike, founded a vast empire stretching from central Asia across the Middle East and North Africa to the Atlantic. With Islam as their national religion and war-cry, and the new empire as their booty, the Arabs found themselves living among a vast variety of peoples differing in race, language and religion, among whom they formed a ruling minority of conquerors and masters. The ethnic distinctions between tribe and tribe and the social distinctions between townsfolk and desertfolk became for a while less significant than the difference between the masters of the new empire and the diverse peoples they had conquered. During this first period in Islamic history, when Islam was purely an Arab religion and the Caliphate an Arab kingdom, the term Arab came to be applied to those who spoke Arabic, were full members by descent of an Arab tribe and who, either in person or through their ancestors, had originated in Arabia. It served to mark them off from the mass of Persians, Syrians, Egyptians and others, whom the great conquests had brought under Arab rule, and as a convenient label for the new imperial people among others outside the "House of Islam". The early classical Arab dictionaries give us two forms of the word Arab—"*'Arab*" and "*A'rāb*" in Arabic—and tell us that the latter meant "Bedouin", while the former was used in the wider sense described above. This distinction, if it is authentic—and there is much in the early dictionaries that has a purely lexicographical existence—must date from this period. There is no sign of it earlier. It does not appear to have survived for long.

From the eighth century, the Caliphate was gradually transformed from an Arabic to an Islamic Empire in which membership of the ruling caste was determined by faith rather than by origin. As increasing numbers of the conquered peoples were converted to Islam, the religion ceased to be the national or tribal cult of the Arab conquerors and acquired the universal character that it has retained ever since. The development of economic life and the cessation of the wars of conquest which had been the main productive activity of the Arabs produced a new governing class of administrators and traders, heterogeneous in race and language, which ousted the Arab military aristocracy created by the conquests. This change was reflected in the organisation and personnel of government.

Arabic remained the sole official language and the main language of administration, commerce and culture. The rich and diverse civilisation of the Caliphate, produced by men of many nations and faiths, was Arabic in language and to a large extent also in tone. The use of the adjective Arab to describe the various facets of this civilisation has often been challenged on the grounds that the contribution to "Arab medicine", "Arab philosophy", etc. of those who were of Arab descent was relatively small. Even the use of the word Muslim is criticised, since so many of the architects of this culture were Christians and Jews, and the term "Islamic", as possessing a cultural rather than a purely religious or national connotation, is suggested as preferable. The authentically Arab characteristics of the civilisation of the Caliphate are, however, greater than the mere examination of the racial origins of its individual creators would suggest, and the use of the term is justified provided a clear distinction is drawn between its cultural and ethnic connotations. Another important point is that in the collective consciousness of the Arabs today it is the Arab civilisation of the Caliphate in this wider sense that is their common heritage and the formative influence in their cultural life.

Meanwhile the ethnic content of the word Arab itself was also changing. The spread of Islam among the conquered peoples was accompanied by the spread of Arabic. This process was accelerated by the settlement of numbers of Arabians in the provinces, and from the tenth century onwards by the arrival of a new ruling race, the Turks, in common subjection to whom the distinction between the descendants of the Arab conquerors and the Arabised natives ceased to be significant. In almost all the provinces west of Persia the old native languages died out and Arabic became the chief spoken language. From late 'Abbāsid times onwards the word Arab reverts to its earlier meaning of Bedouin or nomad, becoming in effect a social rather than an ethnic term. In many of the Western chronicles of the Crusades it is used only for Bedouin, while the mass of the Muslim population of the Near East are called Saracens. It is certainly in this sense that in the sixteenth century Tasso speaks of

> "altri Arabi poi, che di soggiorno,
> certo non sono stabili abitanti;"
> (Gêrusalemme Liberata, XVII 21)

The fourteenth-century Arabic historian Ibn Khaldūn, himself a townsman of Arab descent, uses the word commonly in this sense.

The main criterion of classification in these times was religious. The various minority faiths were organised as religio-political communities, each under its own leaders and laws. The majority belonged to the *Ummat al-Islām*, the community or nation of Islam. Its members thought of themselves primarily as Muslims. When further classification was necessary, it might be territorial—Egyptian, Syrian, Iraqi—or social—townsman, peasant, nomad. It is to this last that the term Arab belongs. So little had it retained of its ethnic meaning that we even find it applied at times to non-Arab nomads of Kurdish or Turkoman extraction. When the dominant social class within the *Ummat al-Islām* was mainly Turkish—as was the case for many centuries in the Near East—we sometimes find the term "Sons or Children of the Arabs" (*Abnā' al-'Arab* or *Awlād al-'Arab*) applied to the Arabic-speaking townspeople and peasantry to distinguish them from the Turkish ruling class on the one hand and the nomads or Arabs proper on the other.

In colloquial Arabic this situation has remained substantially unchanged to the present day, though others have replaced the Turks as the dominant class. But among the intellectuals of the Arabic-speaking countries a change of far-reaching significance has taken place. The rapid growth of European activity and influence in these lands brought with it the European idea of the nation as a group of people with a common homeland, language, character, and political aspiration. Since 1517 the Ottoman Empire had ruled most of the Arabic-speaking peoples of the Near and Middle East. The impact of the national idea on a people in the throes of the violent social change brought about by the entry of Western Imperialism produced the first beginnings of an Arab revival and an Arab national movement aiming at the creation of an independent state or states. The movement began in Syria and its first leaders seem to have thought in terms only of that country. Soon it spread to Iraq and in later years developed closer relations with the local nationalist movements in Egypt and even in the Arabic-speaking countries of North Africa.

For the theorists of Arab nationalism the Arabs are a nation in the European sense, including all those within certain boundaries who speak Arabic and cherish the memory of bygone Arab glory. There are different views as to where these boundaries are. For some they include only the Arabic-speaking countries of south-west Asia. Others add Egypt—though here there was a conflict of opinion with the many Egyptians who conceived of their nationalism in purely Egyptian terms. Many include the entire Arabic-speaking world from Morocco to the borders of Persia and Turkey. The social barrier between sedentary and nomad has ceased to be significant from this point of view, despite its survival in the colloquial use of "Arab" for Bedouin. The religious barrier in a society long dominated by a theocratic faith is less easily set aside. Though few of the spokesmen of the movement will admit it, many Arabs still exclude those who, though they speak Arabic, reject the Arabian faith and therefore much of the civilisation that it fostered.

To sum up then: the term Arab is first encountered in the ninth century B.C., describing the Bedouin of the north Arabian steppe. It remained in use for several centuries in this sense among the settled peoples of the neighbouring countries. In Greek and Roman usage it was for the first time extended to cover the whole peninsula, including the settled people of the oases and the relatively advanced civilisation of the south-west. In Arabia itself it seems still to have been limited to the nomads although the common language of sedentary and nomad Arabians was called Arabic. After the Islamic conquests and during the period of the Arab Empire it marked off the Arabic-speaking ruling class of conquerors of Arabian origin from the mass of the conquered peoples. As the Arab kingdom was transformed into a cosmopolitan Islamic Empire it came to denote—in external rather than in internal usage—the variegated culture of that Empire, produced by men of many races and religions, but in the Arabic language and conditioned by Arab taste and tradition. With the fusion of the Arab conquerors and the Arabised conquered and their common subjection to other ruling elements it gradually lost its national content and became a social term applied only to the nomads who had preserved more faithfully than any others the original Arabian way of life and language. The Arabic-speaking peoples of the settled countries were usually classed simply as Muslims, sometimes as "sons or children of the Arabs", to distinguish them from Muslims using other languages. While all these different usages have survived in certain contexts to the present day, a new one born of the impact of the West has in the last fifty years become increasingly important. It is that which regards the Arabic-speaking peoples as a nation or group of sister nations in the European sense, united by a common territory, language and culture and a common aspiration to political independence.

It is a much easier task to examine the extent of Arabism in space at the present time. The Arabic-speaking countries fall into three groups, south-west Asia, Egypt, and North Africa. The largest Arab land in the first group is the Arabian peninsula itself, most of it occupied by the patriarchal kingdom of Sa'ūdī Arabia, still, despite the intrusion of the oil industry, largely pastoral and nomadic. A republican coup against the monarchy in the Yemen, in 1962, began a civil war which still continues. In 1967 the Aden colony and protectorates became independent as 'The People's Republic of South Yemen,' and in 1968 the first steps were taken toward the termination of the British presence in the

Persian Gulf. To the north lie the lands of the Fertile Crescent, until 1918 provinces of the Ottoman Empire, now the states of Iraq, Syria, Lebanon, Jordan and Israel. It is in these countries that the process of Arabisation went farthest, that the sentiment of Arab identity is strongest. Adjoining Arab Asia, in the N.E. corner of Africa, lies Egypt, the most populous, most developed and most homogeneous of the Arabic-speaking states, with the longest tradition of political nationalism and of separate political existence in modern times. In February 1958 Egypt was joined by Syria in a United Arab Republic, from which Syria withdrew in 1961.

South of Egypt, on the African continent, lies the predominantly Arabic-speaking Republic of the Sudan, which attained its independence in 1956. To the West, the former Italian colony of Libya became an independent monarchy in December 1951; Tunisia and Morocco were both recognised as independent in 1956, and Algeria, after a long and bitter struggle, in 1962. In most of these countries the population is mixed, mainly Arabic-speaking, but with Berber-speaking minorities, especially in Morocco. Some Europeans still remain. These countries have been most affected by European economic, cultural and political penetration, least by the Arab revival. During recent years the nationalist movements in North Africa have become increasingly vigorous. While their objectives are still mainly local, the spread of Arabic cultural influences from the Near East, especially in Tunisia, is producing a greater feeling of kinship with the eastern Arabs. Besides these countries, there are Arab communities living in the former British and French dependencies in Africa, among predominantly negro populations, and small Arab minorities in Israel, Turkey and Persia. The total number of Arabic-speaking people in Asia and Africa is variously estimated at between sixty and ninety million, of whom over twenty-five million live in Egypt and over twenty million in North Africa.

All these countries have much in common. All of them are on the border of the desert and the sown, and have confronted from the earliest times until today the ever-present problem of the encroaching nomad. Two of the most important, Egypt and Iraq, are the irrigated valleys of great rivers, highways of commerce and seats of centralised states from most ancient times. Almost all of them are peasant countries, with basically the same social order and governing classes—though the outer forms and even the social realities are changing as the impact of the modern world affects them separately, at different times, in different ways, at different tempos. All but Arabia itself were won for Arabism and Islam by the great conquests and all have inherited the same great legacy of language, religion and civilisation. But the language has many local differences, and so too have religion, culture and social tradition. Long separation and vast distances helped the Arabs, in fusion with different native cultures, to produce vigorous local variants of the common tradition, sometimes, as in Egypt, with an age-old sense of local national identity. Alongside the conquered peoples, here and there, were those who refused either the conqueror's language or religion or both, surviving among the Arabs as Kurds or Berbers in Iraq or North Africa, Maronites or Copts in Lebanon or Egypt. New sects arose in Islam itself, sometimes through the action of pre-existing cults, leaving Shī'ites and Yazīdīs in Iraq, Druzes in Syria and Lebanon, Zaidīs and Ismā'īlīs in the Yemen. The modern age, by subjecting the Arab lands to greatly differing processes, has brought new factors of disunity, deriving from varying social levels as well as from regional and dynastic interests. But modern developments are also strengthening the factors of unity—the rapid growth of modern communications, bringing the different parts of the Arab world into closer and quicker contact with one another than ever before, the spread of education and literacy, giving greater scope to the unifying power of a common written language and memory; and, most obvious, the new solidarity in opposition to the West and in reaction against Western influence.

One last problem remains to be discussed in these introductory remarks. The European writer on Islamic history labours under a special disability. Writing in a Western language, he necessarily uses Western terms. But these terms are based on

Western categories of thought and analysis, themselves deriving in the main from Western history. Their application to the conditions of another society formed by different influences and living in different ways of life can at best be only an analogy and may be dangerously misleading. To take an example: such pairs of words as Church and State, spiritual and temporal, ecclesiastical and lay, had no real equivalents in Arabic until modern times, when they were created to translate modern ideas; for the dichotomy which they express was unknown to mediaeval Muslim society and unarticulated in the mediaeval Muslim mind. The community of Islam was Church and State in one, with the two indistinguishably interwoven; its titular head, the Caliph, was at once a secular and a religious chief. Again, the term "feudalism", strictly speaking, refers to the form of society which existed in western Europe between the break-up of the Roman Empire and the beginning of the modern order. Its use for other areas and other periods must inevitably, unless it is carefully defined in its new context, create the impression that the type of society thus described is identical with or at least similar to west-European feudalism. But no two societies are exactly the same, and though the social order in Islam at certain periods may show quite a number of important resemblances to west-European feudalism, this can never justify the total identification which is implicit in the unrestricted use of the term. Such words as "religion", "state", "sovereignty", "democracy", mean very different things in the Islamic context and indeed vary in meaning from one part of Europe to another. The use of such words, however, is inevitable in writing in English and for that matter in writing in the modern languages of the Orient, influenced for close on a century by Western modes of thought and classification. In the following pages they are to be understood at all times in their Islamic context and should not be taken as implying any greater degree of resemblance to corresponding Western institutions than is specifically stated.

I

ARABIA BEFORE ISLAM

The burden of the desert of the sea. As whirlwinds in the south pass through; so *it cometh from the desert, from a terrible land.* (*Isaiah* xxi, 1)

THE Arabian peninsula forms a vast rectangle of some one-and-a-quarter million square miles area. It is bordered in the north by the chain of territories commonly known as the Fertile Crescent—in Mesopotamia, Syria and Palestine—and their desert borderlands; in the east and south by the Persian Gulf and Indian Ocean; in the west by the Red Sea. The south-western districts of the Yemen consist of well-watered mountain country which from an early date permitted the rise of agriculture and the development of flourishing and relatively advanced sedentary civilisations. The remainder of the country consists of waterless steppes and deserts broken only by an occasional oasis and crossed by a few caravan and trade routes. The population was mainly pastoral and nomadic, living by its flocks and by raiding the peoples of the oases and of the cultivated neighbouring provinces.

The deserts of Arabia are of various kinds: the most important according to the Arab classification are the Nufūd, a sea of enormous shifting sand-dunes forming a landscape of constantly changing aspect; the Ḥamād, rather more solid ground in the areas nearer to Syria and Iraq; the steppe country, where the ground is more compact and where occasional rainfall produces a sudden and transient vegetation; and finally the vast and impenetrable sand desert of the south-east. Between these zones communications are limited and difficult, depending mainly on wadis, so that the inhabitants of the different parts of Arabia had little contact with one another.

The centre and north of the peninsula are traditionally divided by the Arabs into three zones. The first of these is the

Tihāma, a Semitic word meaning "lowland", and applied to the undulating plains and slopes of the Red Sea coast. The second, moving eastwards, is the Ḥijāz, or "barrier". This term was originally applied only to the mountain range separating the coastal plain from the plateau of Najd, but was later extended to include much of the coastal plain itself. To the east of the Ḥijāz lies the great inland plateau of Najd, most of it consisting of Nufūd desert.

From very early times Arabia has formed a transit area between the Mediterranean countries and the Further East, and its history has to a large extent been determined by the vicissitudes of east-west traffic. Communications both within Arabia and through Arabia have been directed by the geographical configuration of the peninsula into certain well-defined lines. The first of these is the Ḥijāz route, running from the Red Sea ports and the border posts of Palestine and Transjordan along the inner flank of the Red Sea coastal range and onwards to the Yemen. This was at various times a route for caravan traffic between the Empire of Alexander and its successors in the Near East and the countries of Further Asia. It was also the route of the Ḥijāz railway. A second route runs through the Wādī'd-Dawāsir, running from the extreme north-east of the Yemen to central Arabia, where it links up with another route, the Wādī'r-Rumma, to southern Mesopotamia. This was the main medium of contact in ancient times between the Yemen and the civilisations of Assyria and Babylon. Finally, the Wādī's-Sirḥān links central Arabia with south-eastern Syria via the Jawf oases.

Until we can dig for history in Arabia, as we have dug in Egypt, Palestine and Mesopotamia, the early centuries of Arabia will remain obscure, and the searcher in the field will have to pick his way warily among the debris of half-erected and half-demolished hypotheses which the historian, with the scanty equipment of fact that he now possesses, can neither complete nor raze to the ground. Perhaps the best-known of these is the Winckler-Caetani theory, so named after its two most distinguished exponents. According to this, Arabia was originally a land of great fertility and the first home of the

Semitic peoples. Through the millennia it has been undergoing a process of steady desiccation, a drying up of wealth and waterways and a spread of the desert at the expense of the cultivable land. The declining productivity of the peninsula, together with the increase in the number of the inhabitants, led to a series of crises of overpopulation and consequently to a recurring cycle of invasions of the neighbouring countries by the Semitic peoples of the peninsula. It was these crises that carried the Syrians, Aramaeans, Canaanites (including the Phoenicians and Hebrews) and finally the Arabs themselves into the Fertile Crescent. The Arabs of history would thus be the undifferentiated residue after the great invasions of ancient history had taken place. Although no thorough geological survey of Arabia has yet been made, some evidence has already come to light in support of this theory in the form of dried-up waterways and other indications of past fertility. There is, however, no evidence that this process of desiccation took place after the beginning of human life in the peninsula, nor indeed that it took place at a pace great enough to influence directly the course of human affairs. There is also some philological evidence in support of the theory in that the Arabic language, though the most recent of the Semitic languages in its emergence as a literary and cultural instrument, is nevertheless in many ways the oldest of them in its grammatical structure and consequently the nearest to the original proto-Semitic tongue. An alternative hypothesis is that advanced by the Italian scholar Ignazio Guidi, who prefers southern Mesopotamia as the homeland of the Semites and points out that while the Semitic languages have common words for "river" and "sea" they have none for "mountain" or "hill". Other scholars have suggested Africa and Armenia.

The national tradition of the Arabs divides the Arabian people into two main stems, the northern and the southern, This distinction is echoed in the tenth chapter of Genesis where two distinct lines of descent from Shem are given for the peoples of south-western and of central and northern Arabia, the latter of which is closer to the Hebrews. The ethnological significance of this distinction is and will probably remain completely unknown. It first appears in history in linguistic and cultural terms. The southern-Arabian language is different from that of northern Arabia, which ultimately developed into classical Arabic. It is written in a different alphabet, known to us from inscriptions, and is related to Ethiopic, which was indeed developed in Abyssinia by colonists from southern Arabia who established the first centres of Ethiopian civilisation. Another important distinction is that the southern Arabians were a sedentary people.

The chronology of early southern Arabian history is obscure. One of the earliest kingdoms named in records is Saba, perhaps identical with the Biblical Sheba whose queen entered into relations with King Solomon. Saba may have been in existence as far back as the tenth century B.C. There are occasional references from the eighth century and evidence of full development by the sixth. Round about the year 750 B.C. one of the Sabean Kings built the famous Ma'rib dam which for long regulated the agricultural life of the kingdom. Commercial links were maintained with the African coastlands opposite and probably with countries further afield. The Sabeans appear to have colonised extensively in Africa and to have founded the kingdom of Abyssinia, the name of which comes from Habashat, a south-west Arabian people.

From the time when the conquests of Alexander brought the Mediterranean world into contact with the Further East, increased information in Greek sources testifies to a growing interest in southern Arabia. The Ptolemies of Egypt sent ships through the Red Sea, exploring the Arabian coasts and the trade-routes to India. Their successors in the Near East retained that interest. By the end of the fifth century A.D. the kingdom of Saba was in an advanced state of decline. Muslim and Christian sources suggest that it had fallen under the dominance of the Himyarites, another southern Arabian people. The last of the Himyarite Kings, Dhū Nuwās, was converted to Judaism. As a reprisal for Byzantine persecution of the Jews he adopted repressive measures against the Christian settlers in southern Arabia. This in turn produced repercussions in Byzantium and in Ethiopia, by now a Christian state, and provided the latter with the inducement and the opportunity at once to avenge the persecuted Christians and to seize the key to the Indian trade. The Sabean kingdom was ended by a successful Ethiopian invasion with local Christian support. Ethiopian rule in the Yemen did not last long. In A.D. 575 an expedition from Persia invaded the country and reduced it to a satrapy without great difficulty. Persian rule too was ephemeral, and by the time of the Muslim conquest little sign of it remained.

The basis of society in southern Arabia was agriculture and the inscriptions, with their frequent references to dams, canals, boundary problems and landed property, suggest a high degree of development. Besides cereals the southern Arabians produced myrrh, incense and other spices and aromatics. These last were their main export, and in the Mediterranean lands the spices of southern Arabia, often confused with those arriving via southern Arabia from more distant lands, led to its almost legendary reputation as a land of wealth and prosperity—the Arabia Eudaemon or Arabia Felix of the classical world. The spices of Arabia have many echoes in the literature of the West, from the "thesauris arabicis" of Horace to the "perfumes of Arabia" of Shakespeare and Milton's "spicy shores of Araby the blest".

The political organisation of southern Arabia was monarchic and appears to have been solidly founded with regular succession from father to son. The kings were not divine, as elsewhere in the East, and their authority, at certain periods at least, was limited by councils of notables and at a later date by a kind of feudalism with local lords ruling over their vassals and peasants from castles.

The religion of southern Arabia was polytheistic and bears a general, though not detailed, resemblance to that of the other ancient semitic peoples. Temples were important centres of public life and possessed great wealth, administered by the chief priest. The spice crop itself was regarded as sacred and one-third was reserved for the gods, i.e. for the priests. Though writing was known and many inscriptions have survived, there is no sign of any books or literature.

When we turn from southern to central and northern Arabia we find a very different story, based on very much scantier information. We have seen that Assyrian, Biblical and Persian sources give us occasional references to nomadic peoples in the centre and north. The southern Arabians, too, appear to have colonised to a limited extent in the north, probably for trade. Our first detailed information dates from the classical period, when the penetration of Hellenistic influences from Syria and the periodic exploitation of the west Arabian trade-route produced a series of semi-civilised border states in the Syrian and northern Arabian desert marches.

These states, though Arab in origin, were strongly under the influence of hellenised Aramaic culture, and generally used the Aramaic language for their inscriptions. Their Arab character is revealed only in their proper names. The first, and perhaps the most important of them, was that of the Nabateans, which ruled at the period of its greatest power over an area stretching from the Gulf of Aqaba northwards to the Dead Sea and including much of the northern Ḥijāz. The first king known from inscriptions is Aretas (in Arabic, Ḥāritha) who is mentioned in 169 B.C. Its capital was at Petra, in the present kingdom of Jordan. The Nabatean kingdom made its first contacts with Rome in the year 65 B.C., when Pompey visited Petra. The Romans established friendly relations with the Arab kingdom, which served as a kind of buffer state between the settled areas of the Roman east and the untamable desert. In 25–24 B.C. the Nabatean kingdom served as a base for the expedition of Aelius Gallus. This expedition, sent by Augustus to conquer the Yemen, was the one and only Roman attempt to penetrate into Arabia. Its motive was the control of the southern outlet of the trade route to India. Embarking from a Nabatean Red Sea port, Aelius Gallus succeeded in landing in western Arabia and penetrating deep into the interior. The expedition, however, was a complete failure and ended in an ignominious Roman withdrawal.

During the first century A.D. Roman-Nabatean relations deteriorated, and in A.D. 105 the Emperor Trajan made northern Nabatea a Roman province, known as Palaestina Tertia. We may note in passing that the Arabs of the Roman border provinces provided the Roman Empire with at least one Emperor, Philip, who ruled from A.D. 244 to 249. The period immediately after his death saw the rise of the second of the aramaised Arab border states of south-east Syria. This was the famous kingdom

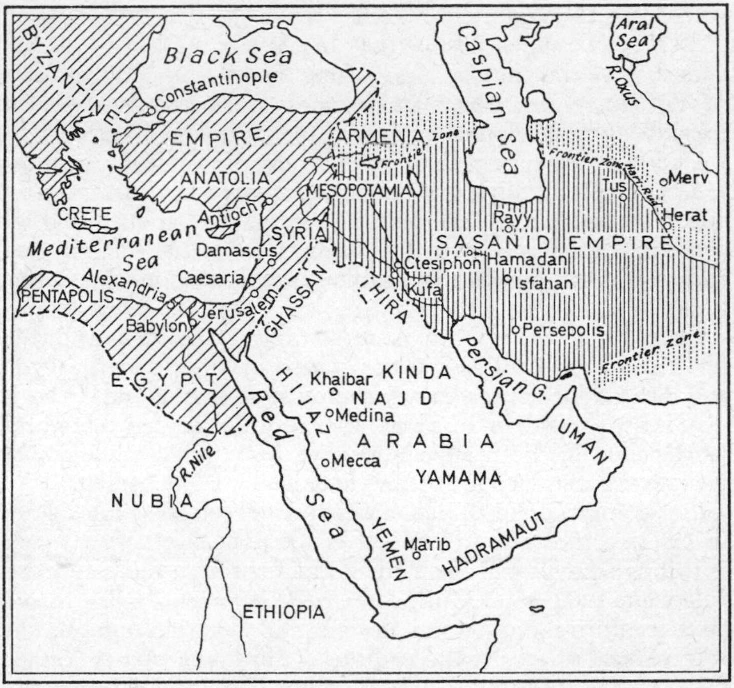

The Near and Middle East on the eve of the rise of Islam

of Palmyra, established in the Syro-Arabian Desert, again at the starting point of the western trade-route. Its first ruler was Odenathus (in Arabic, Udhaina), who was granted recognition as king by the Emperor Gallienus in A.D. 265 as a reward for his assistance in the war against the Persians. After his death he was succeeded by his widow, the famous Zenobia (in Arabic,

Zainab), who for a time claimed to be queen of the greater part of the Near East and proclaimed her son, known to the classical sources as Athenodorus, probably a Greek translation of the Arabic Wahballāt, as Caesar Augustus. The Emperor Aurelian was at last moved to action, and in A.D. 273 conquered Palmyra, suppressed the kingdom and sent Zenobia to Rome in golden chains to figure in a Roman triumph.

These two states, despite their brief blaze of glory in Roman annals, were transitory affairs, lacking the solidity and compactness of the southern Arabian kingdoms and based in the main on shifting nomadic and semi-nomadic peoples. They derived their importance from their position on the trade-routes running from Rome through western Arabia to the further East and from their function as buffer states or tributary border principalities which saved the Romans from the difficult and costly task of maintaining military defences on the desert borders.

Less is known of two Arab states that flourished in the Hellenistic period in the interior. These are the states of Liḥyān and Thamūd. Both are known mainly from inscriptions in their own language and, in the case of the latter, from a few references in the Qur'ān. Both appear to have been for a while under Nabatean suzerainty and to have later become independent.

At some time in the fourth century the trade-routes seem to have been diverted from western Arabia to other channels —through Egypt and the Red Sea and through the Euphrates valley and the Persian Gulf. The period between the fourth and sixth centuries was one of decline and deterioration. In the south-west, as we have seen, the civilisations of the Yemen decayed and fell under foreign rule. The loss of prosperity and the migrations of the southern tribes to the north are telescoped by the Arab national tradition into the single, striking episode of the breaking of the Ma'rib dam and the resulting desolation. In the north the once flourishing border states came under direct Imperial rule or reverted to nomadic anarchy. Over the greater part of the peninsula such towns as existed dwindled or disappeared, and nomadism spread everywhere at the expense of trade and cultivation.

The dominant feature of the population of central and northern Arabia in this crucial period immediately preceding the rise of Islam is Bedouin tribalism. In Bedouin society the social unit is the group, not the individual. The latter has rights and duties only as a member of his group. The group is held together externally by the need for self-defence against the hardships and dangers of desert life, internally by the blood-tie of descent in the male line which is the basic social bond. The livelihood of the tribe depends on their flocks and herds and on raiding the neighbouring settled countries and such caravans as still venture to cross Arabia. It is by a kind of chain of mutual raiding that commodities from the settled lands penetrate via the tribes nearest to the borders to those of the interior. The tribe does not usually admit of private landed property, but exercises collective rights over pastures, water sources, etc. There is some evidence that even the flocks were at times the collective property of the tribe and that only movable objects were subject to personal ownership.

The political organisation of the tribe was rudimentary. Its head was the Sayyid or Sheikh, an elected leader who was rarely more than a first among equals. He followed rather than led tribal opinion. He could neither impose duties nor inflict penalties. Rights and obligations attached to individual families within the tribe but to no one outside. The function of the Sheikh's "government" was arbitration rather than command. He possessed no coercive powers and the very concepts of authority, kingship, public penalties, etc., were abhorrent to Arab nomad society. The Sheikh was elected by the elders of the tribe, usually from among the members of a single family, a sort of Sheikhly house, known as the *Ahl al-bait*, "the people of the house". He was advised by a council of elders called the *Majlis*, consisting of the heads of the families and representatives of clans within the tribe. The *Majlis* was the mouthpiece of public opinion. A distinction seems to have been recognised between certain clans regarded as aristocratic and the rest.

The life of the tribe was regulated by custom, the *Sunna* or practice of the ancestors, which owed such authority as it had to the general veneration for precedent and found its only sanction in public opinion. The tribal Majlis was its outward symbol and its sole instrument. The chief social limitation of the prevailing anarchy was the custom of blood-vengeance, imposing on the kin of a murdered man the duty of exacting vengeance from the murderer or one of his fellow tribesmen.

The religion of the nomads was a form of polydaemonism related to the paganism of the ancient Semites. The beings it adored were in origin the inhabitants and patrons of single places, living in trees, fountains, and especially in sacred stones. There were some gods in the true sense, transcending in their authority the boundaries of purely tribal cults. The three most important were Manāt, 'Uzza, and Allāt, the last of whom was mentioned by Herodotus. These three were themselves subordinate to a higher deity, usually called Allah. The religion of the tribes had no real priesthood; the migratory nomads carried their gods with them in a red tent forming a kind of ark of the covenant, which accompanied them to battle. Their religion was not personal but communal. The tribal faith centred around the tribal god, symbolised usually by a stone, sometimes by some other object. It was guarded by the Sheikhly house, which thus gained some religious prestige. God and cult were the badge of tribal identity and the sole ideological expression of the sense of unity and cohesion of the tribe. Conformity to the tribal cult expressed political loyalty. Apostasy was the equivalent of treason.

The only exception to this nomadic way of life was the oasis. Here small sedentary communities formed a rudimentary political organisation and the outstanding family of the oasis would usually establish a kind of petty kingship over its inhabitants. Sometimes the ruler of the oasis would claim a vague measure of suzerainty over the neighbouring tribes. Sometimes, too, an oasis might obtain control over a neighbouring oasis and thus establish an ephemeral desert empire. Only one such, that of Kinda, need be mentioned, since its rise and expansion in many ways foreshadow the later expansion of Islam. The kingdom of Kinda flourished in the late fifth and early sixth century in northern Arabia. At first powerful, even extending into the area of the border states, it collapsed because of its lack of moral force and inner cohesion and because of its failure to penetrate the barriers erected by the Byzantine and Persian empires, then relatively far more powerful than a few decades later when they faced the onslaught of Islam. The realm of Kinda left a more permanent memorial in Arabic poetry. By the sixth century the Arab tribes of the peninsula possessed a standard and common poetic language and technique, independent of tribal dialects, and uniting the Arab tribes in a single tradition and a single orally transmitted culture. This common language and literature owed much of their impetus and development to the achievements and memories of Kinda, the first great joint adventure of the central and northern tribes. During the sixth century it reached its full classical maturity.

Here and there settled nomads established towns with a rather more advanced stage of society. The most important of these was Mecca, in the Ḥijāz. In the town each clan still had its Majlis and its own stone, but the union of the clans forming the town was outwardly expressed by a collection of stones in one central shrine with a common symbol. The cube-shaped building known as the Ka'ba was such a symbol of unity in Mecca, where a council known as the *Mala*, drawn from the Majlises of the clans, replaced the simple tribal Majlis. Here the conditional and consensual character of sheikhly authority was weakened and to some extent supplanted by a kind of oligarchy of ruling families.

Despite the regression of this period Arabia was still not wholly isolated from the civilised world but lay rather on its fringes. Persian and Byzantine culture, both material and moral, permeated through several channels, most of them connected with the trans-Arabian trade-routes. Of some importance was the settlement of foreign colonies in the peninsula itself. Numbers of Jewish and Christian settlements were established in different parts of Arabia, both spreading Aramaic and Hellenistic culture. The chief southern Arabian Christian centre was in Najrān, where a relatively advanced political life was developed. Jews and Judaised Arabs were everywhere, especially in Yathrib, later renamed Medina. They were mainly agriculturists and artisans. Their origin is uncertain and many different theories have been advanced.

Another channel of penetration was through the border states. The same need as had led the Romans to encourage the rise of the Nabatean and Palmyrene kingdoms induced the Byzantine and Persian Empires to allow the development of Arab border states on the Arabian frontiers of Syria and Iraq. The two states of Ghassān and Ḥīra were both Christian, the former Monophysite, the latter Nestorian. Both had a tincture of Aramaic and Hellenistic culture, some of which percolated to the interior. The early history of Ghassān is obscure and is known only from Arab tradition. Certain history begins in A.D. 529 when the phylarch Ḥārith ibn Jabala (Aretas in Greek) was given new titles by Justinian after his defeat of the Arab vassals of Persia. The Ghassānids resided in the neighbourhood of the Yarmuk river and were recognised rather than appointed by Byzantium. On the eve of the rise of Islam the subsidies hitherto paid by Byzantium to the Ghassānids were stopped by Heraclius as a measure of economy after the exhausting Persian War, and the Muslim invaders consequently found Ghassān in a state of resentment and disloyalty to Byzantium. On the border-lines of the Persian-dominated province of Iraq lay the Arab principality of Ḥīra, a vassal state of the Sasanid Emperors of Persia, dependent when they were strong, self-assertive when they were weak. Its function in the Sasanid Empire was the same as that of the Ghassānids in the Byzantine Empire. In the Persian Wars against Byzantium the Arabs of Ḥīra usually served as auxiliaries. Their period of greatest independence was under Al-Mundhir III, the contemporary and enemy of the Ghassānid Ḥārith. Ḥīra was always regarded by Arab tradition as an essential part of the Arab community, in direct contact with the rest of Arabia. Though a vassal of the Persians, it drew its culture mainly from the west, from the Christian and Hellenistic civilisation of Syria. At first pagan, it was converted to Nestorian Christianity, brought by captives. The ruling Lakhm dynasty was exterminated after a rebellion by the Persian Emperor Chosroes II, who sent a Persian governor to rule through an Arab puppet. In 604 the Persians were defeated by incoming Arab tribes who settled in the region, thus ending the state of Ḥīra and the expansion of Persia in north-east Arabia.

Another source of limited foreign influence was direct foreign rule. The short-lived Abyssinian and Persian dominations in the Yemen and the Persian and Byzantine border provinces of northern Arabia were channels through which some knowledge of the more advanced military techniques of the time became known to the Arabs, and some other material and cultural influences percolated.

The Arabian response to these external stimuli can be seen in a number of ways; materially, the Arabs acquired arms and learned their use and the principles of military organisation and strategy. In the border provinces of the North Arab auxiliaries were subsidised and trained on a large scale. Textiles, food, wine and probably also the art of writing reached the Arabs in the same way. Intellectually, the religions of the Middle East with their monotheistic principles and moral ideas brought a tincture of culture and letters to the Arabs and provided the essential background for the later success of Muḥammad's mission. This response was in the main limited to certain areas, particularly to the sedentary populations of southern Arabia and the Ḥijāz.

Despite the extent and numerical importance of the nomads it was the settled elements and more especially those living and working on the trans-Arabian trade-routes who really shaped the history of Arabia. The successive displacements of these routes determined the changes and revolutions in Arabian history. In the second half of the sixth century A.D. a change of far-reaching significance took place. The Euphrates-Persian Gulf route, hitherto favoured by the commerce between the Mediterranean and the Further East, was rendered difficult by the constant wars between the Byzantine and Persian Empires and impeded by political rivalries, tariff barriers and the general disorganisation due to constant conflict. Egypt, too, was in a state of disorder and no longer offered an alternative route through the Nile Valley and the Red Sea. The traders consequently reverted once again to the difficult, but more tranquil, route from Syria through western Arabia to the Yemen, where Indian vessels came to the Yemenite ports. The Yemen itself had fallen under foreign rule. The Palmyrene and Nabatean kingdoms of the north, whose earlier prosperity had been due to a similar combination of causes, had long since disappeared. The opportunity created was taken by the city of Mecca.

The early history of Mecca is obscure. If, as has been suggested, it is to be identified with the Macoraba of the Greek geographer Ptolemy, it was probably founded as a halt on the southern Arabian spice road to the North. It is well placed at the crossing of the lines of communication southwards to the Yemen, northwards to the Mediterranean, eastwards to the Persian Gulf, westwards to the Red Sea port of Jedda and the sea lane to Africa. Some time before the rise of Islam Mecca was occupied by the north Arabian tribe of Quraish, which rapidly developed into an important trading community. The merchants of Quraish had trading agreements with the Byzantine, Abyssinian and Persian border authorities and conducted an extensive trade. Twice a year they despatched great caravans to the north and the south. These were co-operative undertakings organised by groups of associated traders in Mecca. Smaller caravans were also sent at other times of the year, and there is some evidence of sea trade with Africa. In the neighbourhood of Mecca there were a number of fairs, the most important of which was that of 'Ukāẓ. These were incorporated in the economic life of Mecca and helped to extend the influence and prestige of the city among the surrounding nomads. The population of Mecca was diverse. The central and ruling element, known as "Quraish of the Inside", consisted of a kind of merchant aristocracy of caravaneers and business men, the entrepreneurs and real masters of the transit trade. After them came the so-called "Quraish of the Outside", a population of smaller traders of more recent settlement and humbler status, and finally a "proletariat" of foreigners and Bedouins. Outside Mecca were the "Arabs of Quraish", the dependent Bedouin tribes.

The city government of Mecca has been described by

Lammens as a merchant republic governed by a syndicate of wealthy business men. But this phrase should not mislead one into thinking of organised republican institutions on the Western model. Quraish had only recently emerged from nomadism and its ideal was still nomadic—a maximum of freedom of action and a minimum of public authority. Such authority as existed was exercised by the Mala, a kind of urban equivalent of the tribal Majlis, consisting of notables and family chiefs elected by assent to their wealth and standing. Its authority was purely moral and persuasive, and the real basis of unity remained the class solidarity of the merchants. This solidarity was well exemplified in the struggle against Muḥammad. The commercial experience and mentality of the Meccan bourgeoisie gave them powers of co-operation, organisation and self-control which were rare among the Arabs and of unique importance in administering the vast empire which was later to fall under their rule.

It was in this milieu that Muḥammad, the Prophet of Islam, was born.

II

MUḤAMMAD AND THE RISE OF ISLAM

"*And thus we have revealed to thee an Arabic Qur'ān, that thou mayest warn* Mecca, *the Mother of Cities, and those who are about her; that thou mayest give warning of the Day of Judgment. . . .*"

(*Qur'ān*, xlii, 5)

IN an essay on Muḥammad and the origins of Islam Ernest Renan remarks that, unlike other religions which were cradled in mystery, Islam was born in the full light of history. "Its roots are at surface level, the life of its founder is as well known to us as those of the Reformers of the sixteenth century." In making this remark, Renan was referring to the copious biographical material provided by the *Sīra*, the traditional Muslim life of the Prophet. When the problems of governing a vast empire brought the Arabs face to face with all kinds of difficulties which had never arisen during the lifetime of the Prophet, the principle was established that not only the Qur'ān itself, the word of God, was authoritative as a guide to conduct, but also the entire practice and utterances of the Prophet throughout his lifetime. The records of these practices and utterances are preserved in the form of Traditions (Arabic: *Ḥadīth*), each individual Ḥadīth being attested by a chain of authorities in the form "I heard from . . . who heard from . . . who heard from . . . who heard the Prophet say". Within a few generations of the Prophet's death a vast corpus of Ḥadīth grew up, covering every aspect of his life and thought.

At first sight, the Ḥadīth, with its careful enumeration of its authorities, going back in every case to an eyewitness, would seem to be as reliable a source as one could hope for. But there are difficulties. The collection and recording of Ḥadīth did not take place until several generations after the death of the Prophet. During that period the opportunities and motives for falsification were almost unlimited. In the first place, mere passage of time and the fallibility of human memory are alone sufficient to throw doubt on evidence orally transmitted for over a hundred years. But there were also motives for deliberate distortion. The period following the death of the Prophet was one of intensive development in the Islamic community. A series of new social, political, legal and religious problems and concepts came into Islam from the conquered peoples, and many of the ideas and solutions that resulted were projected backwards into the mouth of the Prophet by fabricated Ḥadīth. The period was one also of violent internal conflict between individuals, families, factions and sects within the Islamic fold. Each of them could find no better way of supporting its case than by producing Ḥadīths attributed to the Prophet and expressing a suitable point of view. To take but one example: the relative positions and importance of the families of Mecca during the lifetime of the Prophet are distorted almost beyond recognition in the Ḥadīth literature by the rivalries of their descendants at the time when that literature was recorded.

The Muslims themselves realised at an early date that many of their Ḥadīths were spurious, and developed a whole science of criticism to distinguish those Ḥadīths which were genuine from those which were forged by pious or impious fraud. Traditional criticism operated exclusively by examining the chain of authorities—rejecting some relaters because of alleged prejudice in their point of view or because they could never have had the opportunity to receive the information which they claimed to pass on. Modern critics have pointed out important defects in this approach. In the first place, it is as easy to forge a chain of authorities as a tradition. In the second place, the rejection of relaters by the touchstone of opinion merely represents the victory of one particular opinion and its adoption as a standard for judging others. Modern criticism has operated rather by subjecting the text of the traditions themselves to historical and psychological analysis. The minute and sometimes even captious criticism of Caetani and Lammens has shown that the entire Ḥadīth literature, of which the biography of the Prophet forms a part, must be treated with caution and reserve, and each individual Ḥadīth weighed and tested before it can be accepted as authentic. More recently, the researches of Schacht have shown that many traditions of apparently historical content in fact serve a legal or doctrinal purpose, and are therefore historically suspect.

The one generally accepted source for the life of the Prophet is the Qur'ān itself, the collection of utterances given by Muḥammad to the people of Mecca and Medina during his lifetime as the direct revelation of the word of God. With the Qur'ān and the limited evidence available from other sources it is possible to reconstruct a biography of Muḥammad which, though by no means as detailed as that of the Tradition and of the earlier European writers who followed it, is nevertheless sufficient to bring out the main significance of his career.

Little is known of the ancestry and early life of Muḥammad, and even that little has dwindled steadily as the progress of Western scholarship has called one after another of the data of Muslim tradition into question. The Prophet seems to have been born in Mecca between A.D. 570 and 580 in the family of the Banū Hāshim, a reputable family of Quraish, though not one of the dominant oligarchy. Muḥammad himself was brought up as an orphan in poor circumstances, probably by his grandfather. He acquired wealth and position by marrying Khadīja, the widow of a rich merchant, several years older than himself. These events are echoed in the verse of the Qur'ān: "Did he not find thee an orphan and give thee a home and find thee erring and guide thee and find thee needy and enrich thee?" (xciii, 6–8). That he engaged in trade himself is probable, though not certain. Mecca was a trading city and the frequent use of commercial metaphors and turns of phrase in the Qur'ān suggests some trading experience. The traditions which tell of trading journeys to neighbouring countries call for reserve. Certainly there is little evidence in Muḥammad's preaching of acquaintance with them. The crucial problem of his spiritual background again raises many queries. It is clear that he was subject to Jewish and Christian influences. The very ideas of monotheism and revelation and the many biblical elements in the Qur'ān attest this. But Muḥammad had not read the Bible. The Muslim tradition tells us that he was illiterate. This may or may not be the case, but his versions of Bible stories suggest that his biblical knowledge was indirectly acquired, probably from Jewish and Christian traders and travellers whose information was affected by midrashic and apocryphal influences. The tradition speaks of certain people called Ḥanīfs, pagan Meccans who were dissatisfied with the prevailing idolatry of their people and sought a purer form of religion, but yet were unwilling to accept either Judaism or Christianity. It might well be among them that Muḥammad's spiritual origins are to be sought.

The Call first came to Muḥammad when he was approaching his fortieth year. Whether it was the culmination of a long evolution or a sudden explosion, as the Qur'ān and tradition suggest, is uncertain, thought the latter seems more likely. The Meccans regarded his early preaching as harmless and offered no opposition. At that stage he probably had no idea of founding a new religion, but merely sought to bring an Arabic revelation to the Arabs such as had previously been vouchsafed to other peoples in their own languages. The Meccan chapters of the Qur'ān are mainly religious and deal chiefly with the unity of God, the wickedness of idolatry and the imminence of divine judgment. At first he won little support, and that mainly among the humbler elements. Among the first converts were his wife Khadīja and his cousin 'Alī, later to become the fourth Caliph. As Muḥammad became more aggressive and openly attacked the existing religion of Mecca, opposition to him and to his followers among the ruling elements hardened. A nineteenth-century scholar endeavoured to present the struggle between the infant Muslim community and the Meccan oligarchy as a class conflict in which Muḥammad represented the under-privileged and their resentments against the ruling bourgeois oligarchy. Though this view exaggerates one particular aspect of Muḥammad's preaching to the detriment of the rest, it contains this much of truth, that his early support was drawn mainly from the poorer classes and that the opposition of the Meccans was largely economic in origin. It was based on two considerations. The first and most important was the fear that the abrogation of the old religion and of the status of the Meccan sanctuary would deprive Mecca of its unique and profitable position as a centre both of pilgrimage and of affairs. The second was the objection to the pretensions of one who did not himself belong to one of the dominant families. If it was economic in its causes, the opposition expressed itself politically rather than religiously, and ultimately drove Muḥammad himself to political action. The last period of his stay in Mecca was marked by a persecution of the Muslims which, if less violent than the Tradition suggests, was nevertheless important enough to cause the flight of a group of converts to Abyssinia. Despite persecution, however, Islam, as the acceptance of Muḥammad's faith was called, continued to gain new adherents. Among the most notable were Abū Bakr, 'Umar, a member of the minor family of Banū 'Adī, whose swiftness in decision and action were of immense value to the struggling community, and 'Uthmān, a member of the house of Umayya, one of the dominant families of Mecca and Muḥammad's sole convert of importance among the ruling class.

The failure to make any important progress against the opposition of the Meccans caused Muḥammad to seek success elsewhere. After an abortive attempt in the town of Ṭā'īf, he accepted an invitation from the people of Medina to transfer himself there.

The city of Medina, some 280 miles north of Mecca, had originally been settled by Jewish tribes from the north, especially the Banū Naḍīr and Banū Quraiẓa. The comparative richness of the town attracted an infiltration of pagan Arabs who came at first as clients of the Jews and ultimately succeeded in dominating them. Medina, or, as it was known before Islam, Yathrib, had no form of stable government at all. The town was torn by the feuds of the rival Arab tribes of Aus and Khazraj, with the Jews maintaining an uneasy balance of power. The latter, engaged mainly in agriculture and handicrafts, were economically and culturally superior to the Arabs, and were consequently disliked. We shall see that as soon as the

Arabs had attained unity through the agency of Muḥammad they attacked and ultimately eliminated the Jews.

The migration of Muḥammad from Mecca to Medina—the *Hijra*, as it is called in Arabic—was a turning point and was rightly adopted by later generations as the starting point of the Muslim calendar. Quraish made no serious attempt to prevent it, and Muḥammad left at his leisure. He invited, rather than ordered, his followers to go and himself stayed until last in Mecca, partly no doubt in order to arrive in Medina not as a lonely and persecuted outlaw, but as the head of a definite group with a certain status. The Medinese had invited Muḥammad not so much as a man of God, but as a man possessed by a spirit of unusual power who might serve them as an arbitrator and settle their internal disputes. Islam was useful to them at first not so much as a new religion, but as a system that could give them security and discipline. Unlike the Meccans, they had no vested interest in paganism and could accept the religious aspect of Islam on approval, provided it satisfied their political and social needs. The full religious conversion of the Medinese did not take place until much later. There were from the first differences of opinion among the Medinese as to whether this "foreign" arbitrator should be called in or not. Those who supported Muḥammad are known to the Tradition as the *Anṣār*, helpers, those who opposed him are given the uncomplimentary title of *Munāfiqūn*, hypocrites. The religious quality of this difference of opinion is a projection backwards of later historians.

The Hijra was preceded by long negotiations and finally took place in the year A.D. 622—the first certain date in Islamic history. It marks the turning point in the career of Muḥammad and a revolution in Islam. In Mecca Muḥammad was a private citizen, in Medina the chief magistrate of a community. In Mecca he had had to limit himself to more or less passive opposition to the existing order, in Medina he governed. In Mecca he had preached Islam, in Medina he was able to practise. The change necessarily affected the character, activities and doctrines of Muḥammad and of Islam itself; the records pass from legend to history.

Muḥammad's rule at Medina began with serious difficulties. His really devoted supporters were few in number, consisting of the *Muhājirūn*, those Meccans who had accompanied him, and the Medinese Anṣār, who had to face the active opposition of the Medinese "hypocrites" which, though mainly political, was nevertheless redoubtable until they were reconciled to the new faith by the tangible advantages which it later brought them. Muḥammad had hoped to find a friendly welcome among the Jews, whose faith and scriptures would, so he thought, cause them to receive the claims of the Arabian Prophet with greater sympathy and understanding. In order to appease them, he adopted a number of Jewish practices, including the fast of Kippur and the prayer towards Jerusalem. The Jews, however, rejected with contempt the pretensions of the Gentile Prophet and opposed him on precisely the religious level where he was most sensitive. They failed in their opposition because of their inner disunity and their unpopularity among the Medinese generally. Muḥammad, realizing that no support was to be received from this quarter, later dropped the Jewish practices that he had adopted, substituted Mecca for Jerusalem as the direction of prayer, and generally gave a more strictly Arabian and national character to his faith.

He had from his arrival in Medina sufficient political power to protect himself and his followers from violent opposition like that of Quraish. Realising that the religious doctrines which were his real purpose needed the support of a political body, he acted politically and by skilful diplomacy converted his political power into a religious authority. An Arab historian has preserved for us a document, most of which is of undoubted authenticity, giving the embryo constitution of the early Medinese community. In the words of the chronicler, "Muḥammad wrote and issued a document among the Muhājirūn and the Anṣār, in which he made an agreement with the Jews and concluded with them a treaty confirming them in the free exercise of their religion and the possession of their goods, imposing on them and conceding to them certain conditions." The document is not a treaty in the European sense, but rather a unilateral proclamation. Its purpose was purely practical and administrative and reveals the cautious, careful character of the Prophet. It regulated the relations between the Meccan immigrants and the Medinese tribes, and between both of these and the Jews. The community which it established, the *Umma*, was a development of the pre-Islamic town with a few vital changes, and marked the first step towards the later Islamic autocracy. It confirmed tribal organisation and customs, each tribe retaining its own obligations and privileges as regards outsiders. But within the Umma all these rights were to be waived and all disputes brought before Muḥammad for settlement. Only Quraish was specifically excepted. No section might make a separate peace with any outside body, and transgressors against the Umma were outlawed.

The Umma supplemented rather than supplanted the social usage of pre-Islamic Arabia, and all its ideas were within the structure of tribalism. It retained pre-Islamic practices in matters of property, marriage and relations between members of the same tribe. It is interesting to note that this first constitution of the Arabian Prophet dealt almost exclusively with the civil and political relations of the citizens among themselves and with the outside.

Nevertheless there were important changes, the first of which was that faith replaced blood as the social bond. Already in the pre-Islamic tribe god and cult were the badge of nationality and apostasy the outward expression of treason. The change in effect meant the suppression within the Umma of the blood feud and the achievement of greater unity within by arbitration. Of equal importance was the new conception of authority. The Sheikh of the Umma, that is, Muḥammad himself, functioned for those who were truly converted, not by a conditional and consensual authority, grudgingly granted by the tribe and always revocable, but by an absolute religious prerogative. The source of authority was transferred from public opinion to God, who conferred it on Muḥammad as His chosen Apostle.

The Umma thus had a dual character. On the one hand it was a political organism, a kind of new tribe with Muḥammad as its Sheikh, and with Muslims and others as its members. Yet at the same time it had a basically religious meaning. It was a religious community, a theocracy. Political and religious objectives were never really distinct in Muḥammad's mind or in the minds of his contemporaries. This dualism is inherent in Islamic society, of which the Umma of Muḥammad is the germ. In that time and place it was inevitable. In the primitive Arabian community religion had to be expressed and organised politically, for no other form was possible. Conversely, religion alone could provide the cement for a state among Arabs to whom the whole concept of political authority was foreign.

The immigrants, economically uprooted and not wishing to be wholly dependent on the Medinese, turned to the sole remaining profession, that of arms. Much righteous indignation has been expressed by European writers at the spectacle of an Apostle of God leading the faithful in predatory raids on merchant caravans; but in the conditions of the time and to the moral ideas of the Arabs raiding was a natural and legitimate occupation, and no discredit attaches to the Prophet for having adopted it. The expeditions against Meccan commerce served a double purpose; on the one hand they helped to maintain a blockade on the city which alone could ultimately reduce it to submission to the new faith. In the second place, they increased the power, wealth and prestige of the Umma in Medina. In March 624, 300 Muslims under the leadership of Muḥammad surprised a Meccan caravan at Badr. The raiders won much booty and their achievements are celebrated in the Qur'ān as an expression of divine good will. The battle of Badr helped to stabilise the community and marked the beginning of a new type of revelation. From then on, the Medinese revelations were very different from those of Mecca, dealing with the practical problems of government, the distribution of booty, and suchlike. The victory made possible a reaction against the Jews and ultimately also the Christians, who were now accused of having falsified their own scriptures in order to conceal the prophecies of Muḥammad's advent. Islam itself began to change. Muḥammad was now quite clearly preaching a new religion, with himself as the "Seal of the Prophets". The new religion was more strictly Arab, and with the adoption of the Ka'ba in Mecca as a place of pilgrimage the conquest of the city became a religious duty.

In March 625 Quraish, reacting against the growing danger of Medinese raiding, sent an expedition against Muḥammad and defeated the Muslims on the slopes of Uḥud. They did not feel strong enough to continue to Medina and returned to Mecca. The Muslim community had suffered no real setback and, as after the battle of Badr, Muḥammad attacked and drove out another of the Jewish tribes. Quraish, however, had not yet given up the struggle. In the Spring of 627 a Meccan army of some 10,000 men advanced to Medina and laid siege to the city. The simple expedient of digging a ditch around it—suggested according to the tradition by a Persian convert—was sufficient to defeat their siege-craft and after forty days the army of Quraish withdrew. This victory was followed by the extermination of the Jewish tribe of Quraiẓa.

In the early Spring of 628 Muḥammad felt strong enough to attempt an attack on Mecca. On the way, however, it became clear that the attempt was premature and the expedition was converted into a peaceful pilgrimage. The Muslim leaders met Meccan negotiators at a place called Ḥudaibīya, on the borders of the sacred territory around Mecca, in which, according to pre-Islamic usage, no fighting could take place during certain periods of the year. The negotiations ended in a ten-year truce and the Muslims were given the right to perform the pilgrimage to Mecca in the following year and to stay there for three days.

There was some opposition among the more enthusiastic Muslims to this apparently inconclusive result. It was deflected by an attack on the Jewish oasis of Khaibar. The Muslim victory in Khaibar marked the first contact between the Muslim state and a conquered non-Muslim people and formed the basis for later dealings of the same type. The Jews retained their land, but paid a 50 per cent tribute. In the following year Muḥammad and two hundred of his followers went on pilgrimage to Mecca, where the growing prestige and power of the new faith brought him fresh converts. Among them were 'Amr ibn al-'Āṣ and Khālid ibn al-Walīd, both of whom were to play an important role in the later Islamic victories. Finally, in January 630, the murder of a Muslim by a Meccan for what appears to have been a purely private difference of opinion served as *casus belli* for the final attack and the conquest of Mecca.

With the capture of Mecca and the submission of Quraish to the Umma of Islam the mission of the Prophet during his lifetime was virtually completed, and in the year of life that remained to him he does not appear to have engaged in any serious activity. The most significant feature of the final year is the reaction of the nomadic tribes to the new community of Medina. In dealing with the tribes Muḥammad found conditions that were wholly unfavourable to him. The system he offered was in every way alien to them, demanding a renunciation of their intense love of personal independence and of an important part of their established code of virtue and ancestral traditions. It is a tribute to the statesmanship of the Prophet that he understood and to a large extent overcame these difficulties. His real and final aim of conversion was never really achieved and even to the present day the Islam of the Bedouin is regarded with some suspicion by those qualified to judge. The immediate and external aim of his diplomacy after the Hijra was the expansion of his own influence to the detriment of that of Quraish. He achieved this by avoiding friction with tribal prejudices, concentrating on military and political affairs in his collective dealings with the tribes, leaving religion to individual conversion. The terms of Muḥammad's agreements with the tribes were always the same—the tribe agreed to acknowledge the suzerainty of Medina, to refrain from attack on the Muslims and their allies and to pay the *Zakāt*, the Muslim religious levy. In some cases they also accepted Medinese envoys. With the remoter tribes Muḥammad treated on a basis of equality, the tribes maintaining a benevolent and expectant neutrality.

After the conquest of Mecca a pro-Muslim movement of a partial and purely political nature began among the more distant tribes. It was a testimony to the strength and prestige of the Umma and took the form of a series of unsolicited embassies to Medina, known to Muslim history as the *Wufūd*. These embassies offered political submission which was understood as such by Muḥammad, though he did accept the opportunity they offered for religious propaganda. The contract that they formed was a political and personal one with the ruler of Medina, which, according to Arabian usage, lapsed automatically on his death. Among the still remoter tribes affected by the civilising influences of Syria and Persia and too distant to feel and resent the force of Muslim arms there were religiously affected minorities. Here it was from these minorities rather than from the tribes as such that the Wufūd came.

On the 8th June, 632, the Prophet died after a short illness. He had achieved a great deal. To the pagan peoples of western Arabia he had brought a new religion which, with its monotheism and its ethical doctrines, stood on an incomparably higher level than the paganism it replaced. He had provided that religion with a revealed book which was to become in the centuries to follow the guide to thought and conduct of countless millions of Believers. But he had done more than that; he had established a community and a state well organised and armed, the power and prestige of which made it a dominant factor in Arabia.

What then is the final significance of the career of the Arabian Prophet? For the traditional Muslim the question scarcely arises. Muḥammad was the last and greatest of the Apostles of God, sent as the Seal of Prophecy to bring the final revelation of God's word to mankind. His career and success were fore-ordained and inevitable and need no further explanation. Only the pious fantasy of later generations of Believers clothed the dim figure of the Prophet with a rich and multi-coloured fabric of fable, legend and miracle, not realizing that by diminishing his essential historic humanity they were robbing him of one of his most attractive qualities.

The West, too, had its legend of Muḥammad, from the preposterous errors and scurrilities of mediaeval polemic and lampoon to the lay figure of Voltaire's "Mahomet". Beginning as a kind of demon or false god worshipped with Apollyon and Termagant in an unholy trinity, the mediaeval Mahound developed in the West into an arch-heretic whom Dante consigned to a not undistinguished place in Hell as a "Seminator di scandalo e di scisma", and finally, after the Reformation, into a cunning and self-seeking impostor. One legend, widespread in the mediaeval West, even described Muḥammad as an ambitious and frustrated Roman Cardinal, who, having failed to obtain election as pope, sought an alternative career as a false prophet. The last traces of Western theological prejudice may still be discerned in the work of some modern scholars, lurking behind the serrated footnotes of the academic apparatus.

The modern historian will not readily believe that so great and significant a movement was started by a self-seeking impostor. Nor will he be satisfied with a purely supernatural explanation, whether it postulates aid of divine or diabolical origin; rather, like Gibbon, will he seek "with becoming submission, to ask not indeed what were the first, but what were the secondary causes of the rapid growth" of the new faith. Muḥammad did not so much create a new movement as revive and redirect currents that already existed among the Arabs of his time. The fact that his death was followed by a new burst of activity instead of by collapse shows that his career was the answer to a great political, social and moral need. The drive for unity and expansion had already found a preliminary and unsuccessful expression in the shortlived Empire of Kinda. The need for a higher form of religion had led to the spread of Judaism, Christianity and the still more significant movement of the Arabian Ḥanīfs. Even during the lifetime of the Prophet his career was paralleled by a series of false prophets among other Arabian tribes in other parts of the peninsula whose activities were in part an imitation, but in part a parallel development.

Muḥammad had aroused and redirected the latent forces of an Arab national revival and expansion. Its full accomplishment was left to others.

III

THE AGE OF THE CONQUESTS

"*You have seen . . . how their greatness dawned by the Call, their Call spread by religion, their religion became mighty by prophecy, their prophecy conquered by Holy Law, their Holy Law was buttressed by the Caliphate, their Caliphate prospered by religious and worldly policy. . . .*"

(Abū Ḥayyān at-Tawḥīdī. *Kitāb al-Imtā' wa'l-Mu'ānasa*)

AT the beginning of the seventh century, the Near and Middle East was divided between the two great rival Empires of Byzantium and Persia. The history of the previous three centuries was largely a record of their struggles. The Byzantine Empire with its great capital of Constantinople was Greek and Christian in culture and religion and to a large extent still Roman in its administration. The main basis of its power was the great plateau of Anatolia, at that time predominantly Greek. To the south lay the provinces of Syria and Egypt. In these, Byzantine authority was threatened in a number of ways. The population—Aramaic in the one, Coptic in the other—was alien by race and to a lesser extent by culture to the Greeks, and their resentments against Byzantine rule and the crushing burden of taxation which it imposed were expressed in the heretical Monophysite churches which were at daggers drawn with the Orthodox creed of the Empire. In Palestine, the Jews, still an important element, if no longer the majority of the population, had suffered even more grievously than the heretical Christians from Byzantine repression, and had little love for their masters. The Persian Empire of the Sasanids presents a certain general resemblance to Byzantium. Here, too, the core of the Empire, was a plateau—Iran—inhabited by a people speaking an Indo-European language, and ruling as a dependency the Semitic and religiously disaffected province of Iraq. But the culture of Sasanid Persia was Asiatic and was indeed an expression of the anti-Hellenistic reaction that had led to the fall of the Parthians. The state religion was Zoroastrianism. The internal structure of the Sasanid Empire was far less stable than that of the Byzantines. Whereas in Anatolia the organisation of the military themes had given the Empire a solid economic and military basis, the Persian Empire at the end of the sixth century had just emerged from a revolutionary convulsion, in the course of which the old feudal structure was broken up and replaced by a military despotism with a mercenary army. But the new order was far from secure and the many discontents of the population produced a series of dangerous religious heresies that threatened the religious and consequently the political unity of the Empire.

Between 602 and 628 the last of the series of Perso-Byzantine wars was fought. It ended in a Byzantine victory, but left both parties exhausted and weak in the face of the unsuspected danger that was about to burst on them from the Arabian Desert.

The death of Muḥammad confronted the infant Muslim community with something in the nature of a constitutional crisis. The Prophet had left no provision for the succession, nor had he even created a council on the lines of the tribal Majlis which might have exercised authority during the crucial transition period. The unique and exclusive character of the authority which he claimed as sole exponent of God's will would not have allowed him to nominate a colleague or even a successor-designate during his lifetime. The later Shī'a tradition of the nomination by the Prophet of his cousin 'Alī, who married his daughter Fāṭima, is certainly a forgery.

The concept of legitimate succession was foreign to the Arabs at the time and it is probable that even if Muḥammad had left a son the sequence of events would not have been different. The fate of Moses supports this view. The Arab tradition that the Sheikh should be chosen from a single family seems to have had little effect, and in any case the claims of fathers-in-law like Abū Bakr, or sons-in-law like 'Alī, can have had little force as such in a polygamous society. The Arabs had only one precedent to guide them—the election of a new tribal chief. The Medinese proceeded to choose one from among the tribe of Khazraj, thus incidentally revealing the imperfections of their Islam.

The crisis was met by the resolute action of three men: Abū Bakr, 'Umar, and Abū 'Ubaida, who by a kind of *coup d'état* imposed Abū Bakr on the community as sole successor of the Prophet. The Meccans and the Anṣār were confronted the next day with a *fait accompli* which they unwillingly accepted. Abū Bakr was given the title of *Khalīfa* or "Deputy" (of the Prophet), usually rendered "Caliph" in European writings, and his election marks the inauguration of the great historic institution of the Caliphate. His electors can have had no idea of the later functions and development of the office. At the time they made no attempt to delimit his duties or powers. The sole condition of his appointment was the maintenance intact of the heritage of the Prophet.

The authority exercised by Abū Bakr differed from the start in several important respects from that of the Arabian tribal Sheikh. He was the head not merely of a community, but of a region. He possessed executive powers and an army and, since the situation that followed his accession demanded political and military action, he assumed a political and military authority which in course of time became an essential part of the office of the Caliph. Two years later, on the death of Abū Bakr, 'Umar, already the power behind the throne, succeeded by nomination without serious opposition.

The first task of the new regime was to counter by military action a movement among the tribes known to tradition as the *Ridda*. This word, which means apostasy, in fact represents a distortion of the real significance of events by the theologically coloured outlook of later historians. The refusal of the tribes to recognise the succession of Abū Bakr was in effect not a relapse by converted Muslims to their previous paganism, but the simple and automatic termination of a political contract by the death of one of the parties. The tribes nearest to Medina had in fact been converted and their interests were so closely identified with those of the Umma that their separate history has not been recorded. For the rest the death of Muḥammad automatically severed their bonds with Medina, and the parties resumed their liberty of action. They felt in no way bound by the election of Abū Bakr in which they had taken no part, and at once suspended both tribute and treaty relations. In order to re-establish the hegemony of Medina Abū Bakr had to make new treaties. While some of the nearer tribes accepted these, the more distant ones refused, and Abū Bakr was compelled to undertake the military subjugation of these tribes as a prelude to their conversion.

The wars of the Ridda, begun as a war of reconversion, developed into a war of conquest which ultimately led far beyond the boundaries of Arabia. The two conquests, on the one hand of Arabia itself, on the other of the neighbouring provinces of Iraq, Syria and Egypt, were simultaneous and interlinked, not successive. The Arabian tribes would probably never have been conquered had not the conquests in the north provided an attractive solution to the internal economic problems of the peninsula. The first northern expeditions were merely raiding parties aiming at plunder, not conquest. The latter only followed when the weakness of the enemy was revealed. From the first, Medinese control was weak and confined to the general direction of policy. With the difficult communications of the time all detail and much of the initiative remained with the commanders and governors on the spot.

One of the key figures of the Arab conquests is Khālid ibn al-Walīd, the chief general of Abū Bakr. After fulfilling orders by restoring the *status quo* at the death of the Prophet, he decided for himself the problem of what to do next by embarking on a programme of military expansion. The real beginning of the Arab conquests is the Battle of 'Aqrabā' in 633 in eastern Najd. The victory proved to the Arabs the capacity of the Medinese Government and the advisability of submitting to it. Thereafter a series of expeditions radiated in all directions.

Between Medina and Syria lay a number of semi-Christianised Arab tribes, providing a definite barrier to an advance from the desert. These are not mentioned by the sources, though they must have played some part, and one can only assume that the cutting off by Heraclius of the subsidy formerly paid to them by the Byzantine Government led them to throw in their lot with the invaders. In 633 Abū Bakr appealed for volunteers for a Syrian expedition and sent several independent forces to Palestine and Syria. The Arabs defeated a small Byzantine force in the following year and made a number of minor raids in southern Palestine but withdrew to the desert to await aid from Medina, while Heraclius mobilised an army. At this point Khālid suddenly arrived from Iraq up the Euphrates via Palmyra and appeared before Damascus in April 634. After looting the town he withdrew and joined the others in the south. The Byzantines meanwhile approached Jerusalem but were defeated by a united Arab force in the battle of Ajnādain. After a series of further Byzantine setbacks and a six months' blockade the Arabs captured Damascus. They at once disbanded and scattered over Palestine while Khālid moved northward. Meanwhile, Heraclius prepared a powerful army, consisting mainly of Armenians with auxiliary cavalry recruited from the tributary Arabs. Surprised by vastly superior forces, the Arabs withdrew from Damascus and concentrated on the Yarmuk river, where in July 636 they inflicted a crushing defeat on the Byzantines which placed the whole of Syria and Palestine at their mercy with the exception of the two fortified Byzantine strongholds of Caesarea and Jerusalem. Once Syria was conquered Khālid was withdrawn and replaced by Abū 'Ubaida—the administrator replacing the general. In 637 'Umar visited Syria and drew up the broad lines of government.

The proposal to raid Iraq came originally from the chiefs of the Arab tribes of the border area, who, finding themselves sandwiched between the Muslims in the south and the Persians in the north, saw as their only way out the acceptance of Islam and a joint attack on the Persian territories. In 633 Khālid raided Ḥīra with a small and mainly locally recruited force. The unexpected success of the raid led to further attempts and ended with a crushing defeat of the Arabs in 634 at the "Battle of the Bridge" by the Persian forces under the Emperor Yazdajird. The Arabs soon organised a new attack and, in the summer of 637, 20,000 Persians were decisively defeated by a far smaller Arab force at Qādisīya. The Arabs followed up their victory by capturing the Persian capital of Ctesiphon, also known as

Madā'in, and occupied the whole of Iraq. A hastily assembled Persian force was easily defeated at Jālūla and the Arab armies pushed northwards through Syria and Iraq to meet in Mesopotamia and complete the conquest of the Fertile Crescent.

According to Arab tradition the invasion of Egypt was begun against the will of the Caliph as an expression of resentment by 'Amr ibn al-'Āṣ at being passed over in Syria. In Egypt, as in Syria and Iraq, the state of the country was favourable. The Copts were intensely dissatisfied with Greek rule and ready to help the invaders. On the 12th December, 639, 'Amr reached the Egyptian frontier town of Al-'Arīsh with a force of 3,000 Yemenite cavalry. He captured it with ease and was encouraged to turn from raid to conquest. After capturing Pelusium (now Faramā), he marched on the Byzantine fortress of Babylon, near the present site of Cairo, and with 5,000 reinforcements from Medina easily defeated the Byzantines in July 640. In the following year the town itself surrendered and only Alexandria remained to the Byzantines in Egypt. After a one-year siege a treaty was concluded between 'Amr and the Coptic Patriarch whereby the city surrendered and the Byzantine garrison withdrew. A Greek attempt at a reconquest from the sea in 645 achieved a temporary success, but was foiled in the following year.

A story common in many books tells that after the Arab occupation of Alexandria the Caliph ordered the destruction of the great library of that city on the grounds that if the books contained what was in the Qur'ān they were unnecessary, whereas if they did not they were impious. Modern research has shown the story to be completely unfounded. None of the early chronicles, not even the Christian ones, make any reference to this tale, which is first mentioned in the thirteenth century, and in any case the great library of the Serapeum had already been destroyed in internal dissensions before the coming of the Arabs.

The advance of the Arabs into the non-Semitic mountain territories to the north and to the east of the Fertile Crescent was far slower and far more difficult. On the Persian plateau resistance continued for many years and the whole of Khurāsān in Eastern Persia was not finally occupied until the reign of

Mu'āwiya. In Anatolia the difficulties proved insuperable, and to the present day the foothills of Taurus mark the northernmost limit of Arabic speech.

The strategy employed by the Arabs in the great campaigns of conquest was determined by the use of desert power, on lines strikingly similar to the use of sea-power by modern Empires. The desert was familiar and accessible to the Arabs and not to their enemies. They could use it as a means of communication for supplies and reinforcements, as a safe retreat in times of emergency. It is no accident that in each of the conquered provinces the Arabs established their main bases in towns on the edge of the desert and the sown, using existing cities like Damascus when they were suitably placed, creating new ones like Kūfa and Baṣra in Iraq, Fusṭāṭ in Egypt, Qairawān in Tunisia, when necessary. These garrison towns were the Gibraltars and Singapores of the early Arab Empire. In them the Arabs built their cantonments and garrison cities and throughout the Ummayad period they remained the main centres of Arab government. These cities—the *Amṣār*, as they are known in Arab history—played a vital role in the establishment and consolidation of Arab influence in the conquered lands. A minority in the provinces as a whole, the Arabs formed the dominant element in the Amṣār, where Arabic became the chief language. They served as markets for the agricultural produce of the neighbouring districts and through them Arabic spread to the surrounding countryside. Soon each of the Arab garrison cities developed an outer town of artisans, shopkeepers, clerks, and workmen drawn from the subject populations, supplying the needs of the Arab ruling class. The movement of the population from the countryside to these towns was helped by the discriminatory taxation against non-Muslim agriculturists and by the fall in prices of agricultural produce which must have resulted from the large-scale free distribution of revenues in kind among the Arab conquerors.

Initially the great conquests were an expansion not of Islam but of the Arab nation, driven by the pressure of overpopulation in its native peninsula to seek an outlet in the neighbouring countries It is one of the series of migrations which carried the Semites time and again into the Fertile Crescent and beyond. The expansion of the Arabs is not as sudden as might at first appear. In periods when the dam holding the Arabs in their peninsula was too strong to allow a direct break-through, the pressure of over-population found partial relief in a steady infiltration of Arab elements into the border lands. There is much evidence of important Arab infiltration during the sixth and seventh centuries, in particular into the Euphrates basin, Palestine and south-east Syria. The Byzantine towns of Bosra and Gaza, to name but two, had important Arab populations even before the conquests, and there can be little doubt that the conquerors found many of their kinsmen already settled in the nearest of the countries they conquered.

The role of religion in the conquests is over-estimated by earlier writers and has perhaps been under-estimated by some modern scholars. Its importance lies in the temporary psychological change which it wrought in a people who were naturally excitable and temperamental, unaccustomed to any sort of discipline, willing to be persuaded, but never to be commanded. It made them for a time more self-confident and more amenable to control. In the Wars of Conquest it was the symbol of Arab unity and victory. That the driving force of the conquests was worldly rather than religious is shown by their outstanding figures—men of the type of Khālid and 'Amr, men whose interest in religion was perfunctory and utilitarian. With few exceptions the truly converted and the pietists played little part in the creation of the Arab Empire.

The Arab historians of later centuries have given us a great deal of detail about the administration created by 'Umar for the new Empire. In the main, however, their story has been revealed by modern criticism and, more especially, by the many contemporary administrative documents that have come down to us from the first century of Islam in the Egyptian papyri, as a projection backwards of the conditions of a later age. The first caliphs were moved in this respect by practical considerations; they themselves felt no need to define terms and functions or to formulate principles, and the study of their measures must be based on simple facts. Their policy was basically determined by the interests not of the subjects of the conquered provinces, but of the Arab-Muslim aristocracy created by the conquests. It was shaped to a large extent by the behaviour of commanders and rulers. At first the Arabs retained the Persian and Byzantine machinery of government with its officials, and even the old coinage. Shortly after the year 640 'Umar, realising the need for new measures, installed a new system, whereby "the whole Empire was put in trust for the Muslim community with the Caliph as sole trustee". The different conquered provinces had different laws and customs. As the Arabs took over the old systems there was no unified law of the Empire. In Syria and Egypt, the surrender had been on terms and 'Umar was compelled to respect local usage. In Iraq, which had surrendered at discretion, he had greater freedom of action.

The Arabs took over only state lands and the lands of enemies of the regime. Other landowners who recognised the new government retained effective freehold rights on payment of certain taxes. The confiscated lands were registered and administered by the state. Muslims were allowed to buy land outside Arabia and many were granted state lands in a form of lease known as *Qaṭī'a* (pl. *Qaṭā'i'*). These concessions might be of cultivated lands or of dead lands, and in the latter case were usually accompanied by state aid in the form of tax remissions. While few such grants were made by 'Umar, many were made by his successors. Muslim landowners outside Arabia did not pay the full land tax, but, after some dispute, paid a much smaller due known as the '*Ushr*, or tithe. Apart from a small religious levy on Muslims all other taxes were paid by the subject non-Muslim peoples. These included the *Jizya* and the *Kharāj*. In later times these terms were differentiated to mean the poll tax payable by non-Muslims and the land tax. Under the early Caliphate, however, while *Jizya* apparently had already acquired the technical meaning of poll-tax, *Kharāj* was still a generic term for any kind of tax, and was used loosely for the collective tribute levied by the Arabs as a lump sum from each region. The Byzantine and other officials were left to assess and raise the money in the old way.

The conquerors did not interfere with the internal civil and religious administration of the conquered peoples, who received the status of *Dhimmīs*, that is, members of the tolerated religions permitted by the law. The change from Byzantine to Arab rule seems to have been generally welcomed by the subject peoples, who found the new yoke far lighter than the old, both in taxation and in other matters. Even the Christian populations of Syria and Egypt preferred the rule of Islam to that of the orthodox Byzantines. A Jewish apocalyptic writing of the early Islamic period makes an angel say to a rabbinic seer: "Do not fear, Ben Yōhāy; the Creator, blessed be He, has only brought the Kingdom of Ishmael in order to save you from this wickedness (i.e. Byzantium) . . . the Holy One, blessed be He, will raise up for them a Prophet according to His will, and conquer the land for them, and they will come and restore it. . . ." We may compare with this the words of a later Syriac Christian historian: "Therefore the God of vengeance delivered us out of the hand of the Romans by means of the Arabs. . . . It profited us not a little to be saved from the cruelty of the Romans and their bitter hatred towards us." The peoples of the conquered provinces did not confine themselves simply to accepting the new regime, but in some cases actively assisted in its establishment. In Palestine the Samaritans gave such effective aid to the Arab invaders that they were for some time exempted from certain taxes, and there are many other reports in the early chronicles of local Jewish and Christian assistance.

The identification of Islam with Arabism by the Arabs themselves is clear from their attitude to the new converts who began to throng to Islam from among the conquered peoples. So unexpected was the idea of non-Arab Muslims that the newcomers could only enter the faith by becoming *Mawālī* or clients of one or another of the Arab tribes. Although the Mawālī were in theory the equals of the Arabs and exempt from most taxes, the Arabs maintained a contemptuously superior attitude towards them and for long tried to exclude them from the material benefits of Islam. The most important of these was the receipt of pay and pensions from the *Dīwān*, the office set up by 'Umar for the distribution of the revenues of conquest among the Arab warriors.

The assumptions of this system were the identity of Arab and Muslim and the maintenance of the religious prestige by which the Caliph exercised his authority. Its breakdown became inevitable when these assumptions ceased to be valid.

On the 4th November, 644, the Caliph 'Umar was murdered by a Persian slave. Realising the danger of civil war that confronted Islam, he appointed on his deathbed a *Shūrā*, or electoral college, consisting of the most likely candidates for the succession, with the injunction to select one of themselves as the new Caliph. There are conflicting reports as to the proceedings of the Shūrā, but the issue was the surprising choice of 'Uthmān ibn 'Affān. 'Uthmān was known to be weak and was even suspected of cowardice, a terrible fault in Arab eyes. His appointment represents a victory of the old Meccan oligarchic ruling class which, though it had accepted the profits of the new religion far more readily than it had ever accepted its Prophet, still despised the former social outcasts who had hitherto dominated in Medina. Despite the efforts of Abū Bakr and 'Umar to associate the Meccans with the cause by appointing them to high offices—as, for example, the choice of Mu'āwiya by 'Umar as Governor of Syria—the oligarchs were still dissatisfied and sought to recover the pre-eminence which they regarded as theirs by right. 'Uthmān, like Mu'āwiya, was a member of the leading Meccan family of Umayya and was indeed the sole representative of the Meccan patricians among the early companions of the Prophet with sufficient prestige to rank as a candidate. His election was at once their victory and their opportunity. That opportunity was not neglected. 'Uthmān soon fell under the influence of the dominant Meccan families and one after another of the high posts of the Empire went to members of those families.

The weakness and nepotism of 'Uthmān brought to a head the resentments which had for some time been stirring obscurely among the Arab warriors. The Muslim tradition attributes the breakdown which occurred during his reign to the personal defects of 'Uthmān. In reality the causes lie far deeper and the guilt of 'Uthmān lay in his failure to recognise, control or remedy them. The wars of conquest which were the main motif of Arab history until the death of ʻUmar suffered a halt after his death. The migration of the Arab people was mainly completed. Masses of Arabs had overflowed and established themselves in the conquered provinces, and the driving force of over-population was for the time spent. Again, the Arabs had come against new and more difficult barriers—the high plateau and unfriendly populations of Iran and Anatolia in the east and in the north, the sea in the west, and the war of conquest became a harder and a slower business. The halt gave leisure to the tribesmen to reflect on hitherto quiescent issues, and soon the forces of nomad centrifugalism produced a collapse of administration and a general explosion. The elements of opposition are already discernible under ʻUmar and may have caused his death. Under the weaker rule of ʻUthmān they came into the open. The revolt against him was neither religious nor personal. It was the revolt of the nomads against any system of centralised control, a revolt not against ʻUmar's state, but against any state. They had retained a nomadic, that is a concrete and personal, conception of authority which regarded obedience as a voluntary offering to an individual. Since ʻUthmān failed to inspire it, they felt themselves free to withhold it.

Although the armed attack on ʻUthmān came from Egypt, the real centre of opposition was in Medina itself. Here Ṭalḥa and Zubair, two disgruntled Meccans, ʻAmr, resentful at his replacement in Egypt by a nominee of ʻUthmān, and ʻĀ'isha, the widow of the Prophet, formed centres of intrigue and conspiracy against the Caliph and were probably not unconcerned in the events leading to his murder. ʻAmr and ʻĀ'isha, realising where events were leading, took the precaution of providing themselves with alibis by departing at the crucial moment, the one for Beersheba, the other for Mecca. ʻAlī's role is not clear. Though himself an obvious candidate for succession, who had already been three times passed over, he does not appear to bear any direct responsibility for the murder, though his inactivity and his failure to use his prestige and standing to prevent it gave an effective weapon to his enemies at a later date.

On the 17th June, 656, a party of mutineers from the Arab

army in Egypt, who had come to Medina to present their grievances, entered the Caliph's quarters and wounded him mortally. The murder marks a turning point in the history of Islam. The slaying of a Caliph by rebellious Muslims established a mournful precedent and gravely weakened the religious and moral prestige of the office as a bond of unity in Islam. Henceforth the only nexus between the government and the tribes was political and financial. Both were irksome.

'Alī was almost immediately hailed as successor in Medina, but even some who had been enemies of 'Uthmān had their scruples about recognising as Caliph one who, though not himself guilty, owed his accession in a large measure to the regicides. Others who had had no love for 'Uthmān were still unwilling to recognise the new Caliph, and a pro-'Uthmān party rapidly developed, demanding the punishment of the guilty. 'Alī was unable to comply and proceeded to raise up for himself a whole series of new enemies by revoking many of the appointments made by the murdered Caliph. The opposition to him began with 'Ā'isha, Ṭalḥa and Zubair, who, with a blithe disregard of their own role in the preceding events, withdrew to Mecca to cry war and vengeance. The triumvirate gathered forces for action against 'Alī and transferred themselves to Baṣra, where they hoped for local support.

In October, 656, 'Alī marched out of Medina at the head of his forces. The event was doubly significant. In the first place, it marked the end of Medina as capital of the Islamic Empire, for never again was a ruling Caliph to reside there. In the second place, for the first time a Caliph was leading a Muslim Army to civil war against brother Muslims.

'Alī and his army went to Kūfa, where, after negotiating with the "neutral" Governor Abū Mūsā, they entered the city amid the acclamations of the populace. From thence he marched against Baṣra and defeated the forces of the triumvirate in an engagement known as the "Battle of the Camel", since the main encounter took place around the camel on which 'Ā'isha, "the Mother of the Faithful", was riding. The battle ended in a victory for 'Alī. Ṭalḥa and Zubair were killed and 'Ā'isha sent back to Mecca.

After a brief occupation of Baṣra, where he failed to win over the population, 'Alī returned to Kūfa, which became his capital. He was now master of the whole Islamic Empire, except for Syria, but despite his apparent strength his position was weakened by the tribal disunity and insubordination of his supporters and by the conflicting councils of the pietists and theocrats who constituted a large part of his following and constantly challenged and questioned his authority. In Syria, Mu'āwiya was in a strong position. He was at the head of a centralised authority—the only one in Islam at the time—ruling over a united and docile province, with a good army, trained and disciplined in the frontier wars with the Byzantines. Morally, too, his position was strong. His title to authority was impeccable, for he had been appointed by 'Umar and confirmed by 'Uthmān, the last universally recognised Caliph. In demanding vengeance for the death of his uncle 'Uthmān he was acting in accordance with an old Arab custom sanctioned by the Qur'ān itself. In the earlier struggle between 'Alī and his opponents he had wisely remained neutral. Even now he advanced no pretensions to the Caliphate, but simply put forward his demand for justice, and by a subtle corollary called 'Alī's title to the Caliphate into question by accusing him of the moral guilt of condoning the regicide. He was supported by the resourceful and cynical 'Amr and by the united forces of the army of Syria.

His first overt act against 'Alī was a forcible refusal to stand down for the Governor whom 'Alī sent to replace him. Forced to act, 'Alī eventually set out with an army and met the Syrian forces near the ruined Roman town of Ṣiffīn by the Euphrates in May 657. The engagement was preceded, as so often happened, by inconclusive negotiations, in the course of which Mu'āwiya demanded the extradition and punishment of the murderers of 'Uthmān and possibly also the abdication of 'Alī and the appointment of a new Shūrā to choose a Caliph for Islam. Eventually battle was joined, and on July 26 the forces of 'Alī gained the upper hand. The Syrians, faced with defeat, adopted the expedient of raising Qur'āns on the points of their lances and crying out "Let God decide." This appeal to arbitration could only refer to the question of the regicides, since they could hardly have hoped to find guidance on the problem of the Caliphate in the Qur'ān. 'Alī saw through the trick, but was forced by the pious party in his own camp to accept a truce. It was agreed that each party should name an arbitrator and that the contending leaders should bind themselves to abide by the verdict. Mu'āwiya nominated as his representative 'Amr—an able negotiator loyal to his cause. 'Alī's followers, interpreting the functions of the arbitrators in a different light, forced him to accept the services of the neutral Abū Mūsā. By this device Mu'āwiya had already won a moral victory, reducing 'Alī in effect from the status of ruling Caliph to that of a pretender. The arbitration rapidly brought further difficulties for 'Alī. An important group of his followers, dissatisfied with this step, revolted against him and had to be forcibly repressed in a bloody engagement. They were known as the Khārijites (*Khawārij*), "those who go out", and were to reappear many times in the later history of Islam.

In January 659 the arbitrators met at Adhruḥ. Arab accounts of their proceedings are hopelessly tendentious, but it is clear that their findings were unsatisfactory to 'Alī and probably involved his abdication. He rejected the verdict and the position was once again much as it had been before Ṣiffīn, except that 'Alī was further weakened by the affair of the Khawārij and by the declining morale of his followers. In the months that followed he suffered still further losses. Mu'āwiya was able to seize the province of Egypt, thus depriving 'Alī of a great source of wealth and supplies, and, while avoiding an engagement, raided and skirmished with impunity in Iraq.

The events of the last year of 'Alī's life are obscure. He may have concluded a truce with Mu'āwiya or may have been preparing a new campaign, but in January 661 he was murdered by a Khārijite called Ibn Muljam. His son Ḥasan gave up the struggle and transferred his rights to Mu'āwiya, who was now hailed in Syria as Caliph and soon generally accepted all over the Empire.

IV

THE ARAB KINGDOM

"'Umar said to Salmān: 'Am I a king or a Caliph?' and Salmān answered: 'If you have levied from the lands of the Muslims one dirham, or more, or less, and applied it unlawfully, you are a king, not a Caliph.' And 'Umar wept."

(Aṭ-Ṭabarī. *Ta'rīkh ar-Rusul wa'l-Mulūk*)

THE situation on the accession of Mu'āwiya presented many difficulties. The administration of the Empire was decentralised and in disorder and the resurgence of nomad anarchism and indiscipline, no longer restrained by a religious or moral tie, led to general instability and lack of unity. The theocratic bond which had held together the early Caliphate had been irrevocably destroyed by the murder of 'Uthmān, the civil war that followed it, and the removal of the capital from Medina. The oligarchy in Mecca was defeated and discredited. Mu'āwiya's problem was to find a new basis for the cohesion of the Empire. His answer was to start the transformation from the theoretical Islamic theocracy to an Arab monarchy, based on the dominant Arab caste.

The Arab historians of later days, writing under the dynasties that succeeded the Umayyads and interested in discrediting the deposed house, refused the title of Caliphate to the reigns of Mu'āwiya and his successors. After the Caliphate of 'Alī they speak of the Kingship (*Mulk*) of Mu'āwiya and the rest of the Umayyads with the sole exception of the pious 'Umar II (717-720), who alone is granted the title of Caliph. For the rest the Caliphate does not resume until the accession of the house of 'Abbās in A.D. 750. While there is more than a germ of truth in this charge of secularisation, it should not be exaggerated. Mu'āwiya and his successors did indeed lay increasing stress on the political and economic aspects of government, but the religious factor, though relegated to the second place, still counted for a great deal. And Mu'āwiya exploited it adroitly by his constant campaigns against the Byzantines, which enabled him to pose as the champion of Islam and leader in the Holy War and to claim and receive the religious loyalty of most of the Arabs.

The process of centralisation which was now necessary if the Arab Empire was to survive involved a number of steps. The first of these was the transfer of the capital to Syria, which remained the metropolitan province of the Empire throughout the Umayyad century. The actual capital shifted frequently. The Umayyads, the chiefs of an invading people whose regime rested on desert-power, built their castles on the verges of the desert and safety. The many buildings that they erected and abandoned are still an invaluable guide to their policies and culture. Mu'āwiya established himself in Damascus, where the central position and old cultural and administrative traditions of the city made it appear possible to set up a government able to control the remoter provinces.

The new moral bond which was to replace the lost religious bond was fashioned from the loyalty of the Arab nation to its accepted head. The sovereignty exercised by Mu'āwiya was essentially Arab. No longer religious, but not yet monarchic, it was a resumption and extension of the authority of the pre-Islamic Sayyid. The Byzantine chronicler Theophanes describes Mu'āwiya not as a King or Emperor, but as a *Protosymboulos*, a first councillor. This is not an inept description of the nature of the authority which he exercised. The chief instrument of his government of the Arabs was the Shūrā, a council of Sheikhs, summoned by the Caliph or by a provincial governor, with both consultative and executive functions. Associated with these tribal councils were the Wufūd, delegations of tribes, together forming a loose structure based largely on the freely given consent and loyalty of the Arabs. Mu'āwiya rarely commanded, but was skilful in operating through the more acceptable processes of persuasion and through his personal ability and prestige. In the provinces his authority was exercised through nominated governors, the most important of whom was the bastard Ziyād, known as "Ziyād, the Son of his

Father", the governor of Iraq, the most turbulent and difficult of the provinces, and of the East.

In its administration the Umayyad Caliphate was not so much an Arab state as a Persian and Byzantine succession state. The old administrative machinery with its staffs and procedure remained intact and Mu'āwiya himself employed a Syrian Christian chief secretary. A vital problem for the stabilisation of the Empire was the regulation of succession. The only precedents available to Mu'āwiya from Islamic history were election and civil war. The former was unworkable, the latter presented obvious drawbacks. The method of hereditary succession was still too alien to Arab ideas to be readily accepted. Mu'āwiya, with characteristic diplomacy, found a compromise by nominating his son Yazīd. The process is a good example of the way in which his tribal parliamentarism functioned. The decision was taken by the Caliph and the Shūrā of Damascus. It was confirmed by consultation with the tribes through the Wufūd, and only then promulgated. The opposition was overcome less by force than by persuasion and bribery.

During the reign of Mu'āwiya the Empire grew steadily. In Central Asia the Arabs took Herat, Kabul and Bokhara. In North Africa they moved steadily westward towards the Atlantic. The war against Byzantium continued without remission and the rapid development of an Arab fleet made possible the first great naval victory over the Byzantines at the "Battle of the Masts" in 655, while Mu'āwiya was still only Governor of Syria. The great military event of his reign was the attack on Constantinople in 670. Although the Arabs succeeded in holding a point south of the city for several years the campaign was ultimately unsuccessful and was given up on the death of Mu'āwiya. The wars with Byzantium served the double purpose of bolstering up the religious prestige of Mu'āwiya and of endowing the Arab army of Syria with superior training, discipline and experience.

In 680 Yazīd succeeded to the Caliphate without serious disturbance. He was a skilled and capable ruler with much of the ability of his father, and he again has been grossly traduced by later Arab historians. His great misfortune arose from the development of events in Iraq. The harsh rule of Ziyād and still more of his son 'Ubaidallah had aggravated the discontents of the Arabs of Iraq with Syrian rule and led to a movement in favour of Ḥusain, the son of 'Alī. In the year 680 Ḥusain and a small group of his relatives and followers were massacred by the Umayyad forces in the battle of Karbalā'. The event had no great immediate political significance; its further consequences were tremendous. The dramatic martyrdom of the 'Alid claimant helped to produce a rapid development of the opposition party to Umayyad rule, centred upon the claims of the line of 'Alī.

In 683 Yazīd died, leaving his infant son Mu'āwiya II as successor. A period of crisis and uncertainty followed, which witnessed the first ominous appearance of large-scale tribal strife among the Arabs themselves. The death of Mu'āwiya II after a rule of only six months was followed by an interregnum and the outbreak of the second civil war in Islam. In Arabia Ibn az-Zubair, the son of the Zubair who fought against 'Alī, put forward a claim to the Caliphate, but forfeited what was probably an excellent chance by his obstinate refusal to leave Mecca and establish himself in Syria. In Syria itself open conflict broke out between the warring Arab tribes which ended in a victory for the Umayyads over their opponents at the battle of Marj Rāhiṭ in 684. Marwān (684–685), a member of another branch of the Umayyad House, was now proclaimed Caliph with effective control of Syria and Egypt. He succeeded before his death in arranging the succession of his son 'Abd al-Malik (685–705), to whom fell the task of restoring the unity of the Empire and the authority of the government and of creating a new state organism to replace the crumbling order of Mu'āwiya I.

The second civil war was more complicated and more dangerous than the first. The disintegrating tendencies were operating on a larger scale and with greater intensity, while a number of new factors had developed which brought with them new problems and new difficulties.

Not a great deal is known of the economic life of the Umayyad period. The Arab sources are late, and in the main confuse the issue by reading into the past the developments of a later period and by their almost unanimous prejudice against the Umayyad House and all its works. The presentation of an ordered account of Umayyad economic life is rendered doubly difficult by the conduct of the Umayyads themselves, who operated in an arbitrary and often erratic manner with little care for precedent or system.

Umayyad society was based on the domination of the Arabs, who formed not so much a nation as a hereditary social caste which one could enter only by birth. They did not pay taxes on their lands, but only a personal religious tithe. They alone were recruited for the Amṣār—they formed the majority of the warriors inscribed on the registers of the Dīwān who received both monthly and annual pensions and allowances in money and in kind from the booty of the conquests and the revenues of the conquered provinces.

Even before the rise of the Umayyads, Arabs began to acquire land outside Arabia. From the time of Mu'āwiya onwards the numbers of such Arab landowners increased steadily. Estates were acquired in two ways—by purchase from non-Arab owners and by grant from the Arab government. The new Arab regime inherited the extensive domain lands of the Byzantine and Persian governments. To these were added the considerable estates abandoned by great Byzantine landowners who fled with the defeated Imperial armies. These, together with waste and uncultivated lands, formed the so-called *Mawāt*, or "dead lands", of the Muslim jurists. In order to ensure the cultivation of these lands and the collection of taxes from them, the Caliphs developed the practice of granting leases, known as *Qaṭā'i'*, to members of their family or other prominent and wealthy Arabs. These leases were similar to the Byzantine *Emphyteusis*, on which indeed they were based. They involved the obligation to cultivate the land within a stipulated period and to collect and remit taxes to the government. Unlike non-Arab landowners and peasants, who were liable for the full rate of taxation inherited from the old regime, these Arab-Muslim landowners paid only the '*Ushr* or tithe. The *Qaṭā'i'* increased rapidly in numbers and came to cover vast areas of the best lands. They could be bought and sold and became in effect complete private property. The holders of *Qaṭā'i'* did not normally reside on their estates but in the Amṣār or in the capital and cultivated their estates with native tenant or semi-servile labour.

The numbers of Arabs who settled in the conquered provinces are not precisely known, but they must have formed a small minority among the native populations. Estimates given for Syria and Palestine vary in the neighbourhood of a quarter of a million towards the end of the first century of Islam. The overwhelming majority of these were soldiers, officials, and other townsmen or Bedouins, and only where there had been pre-Islamic infiltration of Arab settlers does one find any number of Arabs settled on the land. An Egyptian source gives the number of Arab peasants in Egypt towards the end of the Umayyad period as three thousand. Many of the Umayyad princes were themselves great landowners and some of them devoted great care and attention to the development of their estates. Ibn 'Āmir, a well-known and successful landowner, attributes to the Prophet the Ḥadīth "whoever is killed defending his property is a martyr". The authenticity of such a Ḥadīth is extremely doubtful, but it well exemplifies the outlook that had developed among the new class of wealthy landlords who formed a dominant element within the Arab ruling class itself.

The great fortunes acquired by some of the Arab conquerors do not appear to have been created by investment or trade, and even the merchant class of Mecca with some exceptions seems to have abandoned its former vocation for the role of a warrior aristocracy. But the Umayyad Caliphs themselves and many other wealthy men lived in great luxury in the cities and even in the desert, and spent vast sums on building, furnishing and textiles. The economy of the time was predominantly, though not purely, monetary. Soldiers and officials were paid in money as well as in kind. Taxes were collected in the same way. The survival of numbers of coins from the early Caliphate confirms the evidence of the historians that the mints taken over from the Persian and Byzantine administrations continued to produce gold and silver currency in sufficient quantities to make this possible.

The disposal by the Arab ruling caste of vast sums of money helped the growth of a new class—the *Mawālī* (singular *Mawlā*), A Mawlā was any Muslim who was not a full member by descent of an Arab tribe. They thus included Persian, Aramaean, Egyptian, Berber and other non-Arab converts to Islam, as well as some of Arabic speech and Arabian provenance who for one reason or another had lost or failed to obtain full membership of the dominant caste. The term did not include non-Muslims, who were known as *Dhimmīs*, that is, followers of the protected religions enjoying the tolerance of the Muslim state in return for the acceptance of a higher rate of taxation and of certain social disabilities.

The Mawālī flocked in large numbers to the Arab Amṣār, in each of which they rapidly built up a large outer town of workmen, artisans, shopkeepers, merchants and others serving the needs of the Arab aristocracy. As Muslims they were theoretically the equals of the Arabs, and claimed economic and social equality with them. This equality was never fully conceded by the Arab aristocracy during the Umayyad period. While some Mawālī landowners did succeed in obtaining a Muslim rate of tax assessment by their services to the new regime, the majority failed, and by the time of 'Abd al-Malik the Muslim government actually resorted to discouraging conversion and driving the Mawālī from the towns back to their fields in order to restore the falling revenues of the state. The Mawālī did indeed fight alongside the Arabs in the armies of Islam, more especially in the border provinces of Khurāsān and the far west. They fought, however, as infantry, with a lower rate of pay and booty than the Arab cavalry. The social inferiority of the Mawālī emerges very clearly from the Arabic literature of the time. A marriage, for example, between a full-blooded Arab woman and a Mawlā was regarded as an appalling mesalliance, and one Arab writer wonders whether such unions would be tolerated even among the Blessed in Paradise.

The Mawālī increased rapidly in numbers and soon outnumbered the Arabs themselves. Their mass settlement in the garrison towns formed a discontented and dangerous urban population, increasingly conscious of its growing political significance, its cultural superiority and its growing share even in military operations. The main grievance was economic. The whole structure of the Arab state was based on the assumption that a minority of Arabs would rule a majority of tax-paying non-Muslims. The economic equalization of the Mawālī would have meant a simultaneous decrease of revenue and increase in expenditure. That could only have resulted in complete breakdown. The division between the dominant caste and the Mawālī, though it coincided to a large extent with the racial boundary between Arab and non-Arab, was nevertheless basically economic and social rather than national. The poorer Arabs of Iraq and Baḥrain, not inscribed on the Dīwān, were forced down to the level of the Mawālī, and shared their grievances. Many of the old Persian squirearchy adapted themselves to the new order.

The discontents of the Mawālī found a religious expression in the movement known as the Shī'a (from *Shī'atu 'Alī*, the party of 'Alī). Shī'ism began as a purely Arab and purely political faction grouped around the claims of 'Alī and of his descendants to the Caliphate. The transfer of the capital by 'Alī to Kūfa and its subsequent transfer by the Umayyads to Syria brought Shī'ism support from Iraqi local patriotism. The real development of the movement began after the martyrdom of Karbalā', when, having failed as an Arab party, it sought victory as an Islamic sect. The Shī'ite propagandists appealed with great success to the discontented masses and especially to the Mawālī, to whom the idea of a legitimate succession in the line of the Prophet had a far greater appeal than to the Arabs themselves. Shī'ism became essentially the expression in religious terms of opposition to the state and the established Order, acceptance of which meant conformity to the Sunnī, or orthodox Islamic doctrine.

This opposition was by no means confined to non-Arabs. In the turbulent garrison cities, and especially in Kūfa, the birthplace of revolutionary Shī'ism, Arabs played an important and at first a predominant part. It was Arabs who first brought

Shī'ism into Persia, where the Arab garrison city of Qumm, a colony from Kūfa, was one of the main Shī'ite strongholds. The opposition expressed by Shī'ism was a social revolt against the Arab aristocracy, along with their creed, their state and their hangers-on rather than a national revolt against the Arabs.

Nor were the supporters of the regime exclusively Arab. The surviving Persian feudal aristocracy, retaining its economic and social functions and privileges, resigned itself to the temporary eclipse of its political rights, and co-operated with the Arab state as long as that state recognised its privileges. On conversion it exchanged a Zoroastrian for a Muslim orthodoxy. The Islamised Persian townsfolk and peasants, still fighting the same enemy, exchanged their Zoroastrian for Islamic heresies, directed against the dominant aristocracy, Arab and Persian.

As might be expected, the Mawālī—Persians and others—were attracted more especially by the more extreme and uncompromising forms of Shī'ism, to which they brought many new religious ideas derived from their previous Christian, Jewish and Persian backgrounds. Perhaps the most important of these is the concept of the *Mahdī*, the "rightly guided one". The Mahdī began as a purely political leader, but rapidly developed into a Messianic religious pretender. The first characteristic appearance of the doctrine was in the revolt of Mukhtār, who in 685–7 organised a revolt in Kūfa in the name of Muḥammad ibn al-Ḥanafīya, a son of 'Alī by a wife other than Fāṭima. Mukhtār appealed primarily to the Mawālī, and it is interesting to note that according to an Arab chronicler the Arabs reproached Mukhtār for raising up "our Mawālī, who are booty which God has granted to us along with all these lands". After the death of Muḥammad ibn al-Ḥanafīya, his followers preached that he was not really dead, but had gone into concealment in the mountains near Mecca and would in his own good time return to the world and establish a reign of justice on earth. The revolt of Mukhtār foundered in blood, but the Messianic idea that he had launched took a firm hold, and during the remaining years of the Umayyad Caliphate many 'Alid and pseudo-'Alid pretenders, both of the line of Muḥammad ibn al-Ḥanafīya and of the line of Fāṭima, claimed the allegiance of the Muslims as the sole righteous sovereign of Islam. One after another of these Messianic rebels followed his predecessors into eschatological concealment, and by his career and failure enriched the Mahdī legend with some new detail. Broadly speaking, the pretenders of the line of Fāṭima represented the moderate wing within the Shī'a, with considerable support among discontented elements of the Arabs themselves. The line of Muḥammad ibn al-Ḥanafīya was associated with extremism both of belief and action and represented more closely the urgent resentments of the Mawālī.

While the Umayyads had to face the mounting discontents of their subjects they could by no means rely on the undivided support of the Arabs themselves. The general tribal sense of independence, still strong among the nomad Arabs, and not so much anti-Umayyad as anti-state, found political and religious expression in a series of movements. In Mecca and Medina the pietists, who had never really accepted Mu'āwiya's compromise of Arabism and centralisation, formed a theocratic opposition stressing the voluntary and religious aspects of the patriarchal Caliphate which they held forth as an ideal. Their anti-Umayyad bias colours the whole of early Islamic religious and historical writing, of which they were at that time laying the foundations. Their opposition to the Umayyads rarely took the form of an armed revolt, but their continuous propaganda helped to undermine the authority of the central government.

An even more dangerous expression of the desire to reject the centralised state and return to a pre-Islamic order with Islamic trappings was the movement of the Khawārij. As we have seen, these were a group of supporters of 'Alī who had rebelled against the arbitration agreement at Ṣiffīn and had demanded a solution by God, that is to say, by arms. 12,000 men withdrew from 'Alī's forces. He persuaded them to rejoin him for a while, but some 4,000 seceded again and 'Alī was forced to attack them and kill large numbers of them in the battle of Nahrawān in 658. The Khārijite movement was at first purely religious, but it gradually developed into an aggressive anarchist opposition acknowledging no authority but that of a Caliph whom they themselves selected and whom they could, and frequently did, at any time reject. In the twenty years that followed the death of ʿAlī a number of minor Khārijite outbreaks took place in Iraq, culminating in a revolt in force on the death of Yazīd. The Khawārij failed because of the fissiparous character of the movement and its tendency to internal conflict and disorder. Under ʿAbd al-Malik the Khawārij were crushed in Iraq and gradually driven into Persia. They were pretty well eliminated by the beginning of the eighth century. They represent the pre-Islamic Arab doctrine of government by consent and the supremacy of private judgment in an extreme form. Their tenets have been well described as "the natural insubordination of the Arabs, rationalised, systematised, exacerbated, and fanaticised by religious teaching".

The main internal weakness of the Umayyad order and that on which it ultimately fell was the recurrent feuds of the Arab tribes themselves. The Arab national tradition divides the tribes into two main groups, the northern and the southern, each with an elaborate genealogical tree showing the interrelation of the different tribes within the group and their descent from a common ancestor. There had been inter-tribal feuds in pre-Islamic Arabia, but they were between neighbouring tribes, often related to one another. The development of feuds between great leagues of tribes was the result of the conquests. In the Amṣār the Arabs were settled in quarters according to their tribes. These segments formed themselves into leagues of rival factions, not on a geographical basis but rather like a mosaic. The tribal trees of Arab tradition are probably fictitious, but are historically significant in that they dominated the Arab life of Umayyad times. The first vague appearance of a feud between the northern and southern "leagues" dates from the time of Muʿāwiya and thereafter grew rapidly, breaking out into open violence whenever the authority of the central government was weakened. This occurred on the death of Yazīd when Qais, one of the chief northern tribes, refused to recognise his successor, opting for Ibn az-Zubair. The Umayyads, with the support of the southern tribe of Kalb, were able to defeat them in the victory of Marj Rāhiṭ, but the Umayyad House had lost its neutrality and descended into the *mêlée*. After 'Abd al-Malik the Caliphs usually relied on one side or the other, and the Caliphate itself degenerated into a party appointment in the tribal conflict. The suggestion has been made that so deep-rooted and persistent a struggle must have had more serious causes than the imaginary genealogies of Arab tradition. These causes have been found in the conflict of interests between those Arabs who had infiltrated into the conquered territories before the conquests—most of them of southern origin—and the predominantly northern Arabs who came with the armies of Islam. This diagnosis is supported by the fact that the southern tribes were generally more open to Shī'a propaganda, suggesting some community of interests with the Mawālī.

The main field of conflict in the second civil war was Iraq, where all the factors were present and active. Kūfa, a growing and important town, was the chief centre and saw a series of convulsions. The early years of 'Abd al-Malik's reign were occupied mainly with restoring order among the Arabs, settling the affairs of the dynasty and establishing peace on the northern border by agreement with the Byzantine Emperor. By the year 690 he was ready for action against the rebels, and within three years succeeded in winning general acknowledgment.

His problem now was to devise a new organisation. The inevitable answer was a greater degree of centralisation, concentrating authority in the ruler and basing it on the military power of the army of Syria. The Caliphate of 'Abd al-Malik was still not an autocracy of the old oriental type, but rather a centralised monarchy, modified by Arab tradition and by the remnants of the theocratic idea. During the reign of 'Abd al-Malik a process known to the Arab historians as "organisation and adjustment" was begun. The old Byzantine and Persian systems of administration, hitherto retained in the various provinces, were gradually replaced by a new Arab imperial system with Arabic as the official language of administration and accountancy. In 696 an Arabic coinage was instituted in place of the imitations of Byzantine and Persian coins hitherto in use. 'Abd al-Malik and his advisers were also responsible for beginning a process of fiscal rationalisation which under his successors crystallised into a new and specifically Islamic system of taxation. He bequeathed to his successor a peaceful and powerful empire enriched by great efforts expended in public works and reconstruction. But the main problems had been shelved, not solved.

The reign of Walīd (705–715) was in many ways the supreme point of Umayyad power. The main interest of the period lies in a resumption of conquest and expansion, now extended to three new areas. In central Asia Qutaiba ibn Muslim, a nominee of Al-Ḥajjāj, 'Abd al-Malik's governor of Iraq, was the first to establish Arab power firmly in the lands beyond the Oxus, occupying Bokhara and Samarqand, and achieving resounding victories. Further to the south, an Arab force occupied the Indian province of Sind. This action was not followed up and the Muslim conquest of India was not to come until a much later date. More important was the landing in Spain in the year 710, rapidly followed by the occupation of the greater part of the Iberian peninsula.

During the reign of Sulaimān (715–717) a great but unsuccessful expedition was launched against Constantinople, the last assault by the Arabs in the grand style. Its failure brought a grave moment for Umayyad power. The financial strain of equipping and maintaining the expedition caused an aggravation of the fiscal and financial oppression which had already aroused such dangerous opposition. The complete destruction of the fleet and army of Syria at the sea walls of Constantinople deprived the regime of the chief material basis of its power. At this critical moment Sulaimān on his deathbed nominated as his successor the pious 'Umar ibn 'Abd al-'Azīz, who more than any other of the Umayyad princes was fitted for the task of reconciliation which alone could save the Umayyad state.

'Umar's task was to maintain the unity of the Arabs and the Arab empire by conciliating the Mawālī. He attempted to do it by a series of fiscal measures which, though they ultimately collapsed, did succeed in tiding over the crisis. The main problem before him arose from the fact that the mass conversion of the Dhimmīs to Islam and the steady increase in the number of Arab landowners combined to produce an increasing number of people refusing to pay any but the lower rate Muslim taxes. Ḥajjāj's remedy, driving the Mawālī back to their lands and demanding the full rate of taxation from all Muslim landowners, had produced resentment and exasperation and was clearly unworkable. 'Umar II tried to meet these difficulties by an arrangement whereby Muslim landowners paid only 'Ushr and not Kharāj, the higher rate of taxation, but no transfers of tribute-paying land to Muslims after the year 100 A.H. (A.D. 719) would be recognised. Thereafter by a legal fiction Muslims could only rent such land and would have to pay the Kharāj on it. In order to pacify the Mawālī he allowed them to settle in the garrison cities without impediment and freed them from both Kharāj and Jizya, the meaning of which was now becoming specialised to the poll tax payable by non-Muslims. Except in Khurāsān, however, they still received a lower rate of pay than the Arab warriors. For the Arabs themselves he granted the equalisation of rates of pay at the Syrian level, hitherto higher than elsewhere, and pensions to the wives and children of warriors. These measures were accompanied by a severer policy towards the Dhimmīs, who were now to be excluded from the administration in which they had hitherto served in large numbers and subjected more rigorously to the social and financial disabilities imposed upon them by law.

The reforms of 'Umar II at once increased expenditure and decreased revenue. His refusal to employ Dhimmīs in the administration led to confusion and disorder, and under the reigns of his successors, Yazīd II (720–724) and Hishām (724–743), a new system was worked out which remained in force with but few changes for long after the fall of the Umayyads. The whole oriental tradition is unanimous in describing Hishām as a miserly and grasping ruler, interested above all else in the collection of taxes. The evidence available does not allow a general statement on the fiscal policy of the Caliphate as a whole. We have, however, some information about the policies of Hishām's three chief provincial governors, 'Ubaidullah ibn al-Ḥabḥāb in Egypt, Khālid al-Qasrī in Iraq, and Naṣr ibn

Sayyār in Khurāsān, and from these it is possible to reconstruct a general picture of the policy of the later Umayyad period. The main basis of the new order was the legal fiction that the land and not the landowner paid Kharāj. From this time on all land assessed as Kharāj land paid the full rate irrespective of the religion or nationality of its owner. The 'Ushr land formed under the early Caliphate continued to pay the lower rate, but could no longer be added to. The Dhimmīs in addition paid the Jizya, or poll tax. The working of this new system, which was to become the canonical system of Islamic jurisprudence, was made more effective by the appointment of separate financial superintendents alongside the provincial governors with the task of carrying out a survey and a census as the basis of the new assessments.

After the death of Hishām the Arab Kingdom declined rapidly to its fall. A violent intensification of tribal strife and the reappearance of active Shī'ite and Khārijite opposition developed so far that by 744 the right of the central government was challenged even in Syria and disregarded elsewhere. The last of the Umayyads, Marwān II (744–750), was a clever and capable ruler, but he had come too late to save the dynasty.

The end came from the party which called itself the Hāshimīya. Abū Hāshim, a son of the Muḥammad ibn al-Ḥanafīya for whom Mukhtār had fought, had been at the head of an extremist Shī'ite sect with Mawlā support. On his death in 716 without male issue his succession was claimed by Muḥammad ibn 'Alī ibn al-'Abbās, the descendant of an uncle of the Prophet. Muḥammad was accepted by the sect and thus obtained control of its propagandist and revolutionary machine. Its main centre of activity was in Khurāsān, in which Arab colonies, chiefly from Baṣra, had settled round about the year 670. They brought with them their tribal conflicts which developed and expanded in the new surroundings. The Arabs were a small minority among a Persian population warlike in temperament and discontented with its social and economic inferiority.

Hāshimite propaganda was launched from Kūfa, in about 718, with a strong appeal to those who believed that the family of the Prophet were the rightful leaders of Islam, and would inaugurate a new era of justice. At first addressed by Arabs to Arabs, the Hāshimite mission soon attracted many Mawālī. A missionary called Khidāsh taught extremist doctrines and won some initial success, but he was captured and executed in 736. Muḥammad ibn 'Alī ibn al-'Abbās disavowed him and his teachings, and entrusted the control of the mission in Khurāsān to a southern Arab called Sulaimān ibn Kathīr, aided by a council of twelve. A period of inactivity followed, during which Muḥammad died and was succeeded by his son Ibrāhīm, whose claims were accepted by the organisation in the east. In 745, Ibrāhīm sent Abū Muslim, a Mawlā of Iraq, as his confidential agent and propagandist in Khurāsān. Abū Muslim achieved considerable success among the Arab and Persian population, including even the rural aristocracy. Despite some suspicion and dissatisfaction on the part of the moderate Shī'a, the leadership of Abū Muslim was generally accepted, and in 747 the Hāshimite putsch began, and the black flags of the 'Abbāsids were raised in Khurāsān. Black has often been represented as the particular colour of the House of 'Abbās. In point of fact, the use of black banners was an attempt to meet one of the requirements of the Messianic and eschatological prophecies, many of which were circulating among the discontented populations of the Arab Kingdom. Other rebels before the 'Abbāsids had raised the black banners. It was only the success of the latter which made them the characteristic of the new ruling house. Within a few years the 'Abbāsids came to be known both in Byzantium and in far-away China as the "black-robed ones".

The rest of the story is soon told. The conflict between the Arab tribes themselves in Khurāsān prevented them from offering any effective resistance to the new movement until it was too late. Once established in the east, the armies of Abū Muslim swept rapidly westwards and the last forces of the Umayyads were defeated in the battle of the Great Zāb. The Umayyad House and the Arab Kingdom had gone. In their place the 'Abbāsid Abū'l-'Abbās, who had succeeded his brother Ibrāhīm as leader of the party, was proclaimed as Caliph, with the title Saffāḥ.

V

THE ISLAMIC EMPIRE

"*A goodly place, a goodly time.*
For it was in the golden prime
Of good Haroun Alraschid."
(Tennyson. *Recollections of the Arabian Nights*)

THE replacement of the Umayyads by the 'Abbāsids in the headship of the Islamic community was more than a mere change of dynasty. It was a revolution in the history of Islam, as important a turning point as the French and Russian revolutions in the history of the West. It came about not as the result of a palace conspiracy or *coup d'état*, but by the action of an extensive and successful revolutionary propaganda and organisation, representing and expressing the dissatisfactions of important elements of the populations with the previous regime and built up over a long period of time. Like most revolutionary movements it was a coalition of different interests, held together by a common desire to overthrow the existing order, but doomed to break up into conflicting groups once victory was obtained. One of the first tasks of the victorious 'Abbāsids was to crush the disappointed extremist wing of the movement which had brought them to power. Abū Muslim, the chief architect of the revolution, and several of his companions were executed and an *émeute* by their followers suppressed.

But what was the nature of this revolution—who were the revolutionaries, and what did they seek to win? Nineteenth-century European orientalists, misled by the racial theories of Gobineau and others, explained the conflict between the Umayyads and the 'Abbāsids and indeed the whole religious schism in early Islam in terms of a racial conflict between the semitism of Arabia and the aryanism of Iran. They regarded the victory of the 'Abbāsids as a victory of the Persians over the Arabs, establishing under the cloak of a Persianised Islam a new Iranian Empire in place of the fallen Arab kingdom. For this view there is some support in the Arabic sources—"The Empire of the sons of 'Abbās was Persian and Khurāsānian, that of the sons of Marwān Umayyad and Arab", says the ninth-century Arabic essayist Jāḥiẓ. But recent research has shown that although racial antagonisms played their part in the agitation that led to the overthrow of the Umayyads, they were not the chief motivating forces of the revolution, and the victors, though including many Persians, did not achieve their victory as Persians nor defeat their enemies as Arabs. The forces of the revolution included many Arabs, especially of the southern tribes, less firmly established in the aristocracy of the conquerors. The Mawālī, who provided the main support of the movement, were not by any means exclusively Persian, but included Iraqis, Syrians, Egyptians and even Arabs who were not full members of the tribal aristocracy. The Persian squirearchy of *Dihqāns*, like the ex-Byzantine official classes in the western provinces, had adapted themselves to the Umayyad regime and played an important part in its working. It was they who assessed and collected the block tributes demanded by the Arabs from each province, no doubt exempting themselves in the process.

It is in the social and economic discontents of the underprivileged town population, especially the Mawālī merchants and artisans who throve in the garrison cities established by the Arabs, that the driving force of the revolution must be sought. The cessation of the wars of conquest, the sole productive activity of the Arab aristocracy who were the ruling class of the Umayyad kingdom, made that class historically redundant, and the way was open for the establishment of a new social order based on a peace economy of agriculture and trade and with a cosmopolitan ruling class of officials, merchants, bankers, landowners and the 'Ulamā', the class of religious scholars, jurists, teachers and dignitaries who were the nearest Islamic approach to a priesthood. The task was made easier by the political ineptitude and inner dissensions of the Arabs themselves and by the defection of many of them to the revolutionary movement.

The nature of the movement can be seen most clearly in

the changes that followed its victory. The first and most obvious of these was the transfer of the centre of gravity from Syria to Iraq, the traditional centre of the great cosmopolitan Empires of the Near and Middle East. The first 'Abbāsid Caliph Saffāḥ (750–754) set up his capital in the small town of Hāshimīya, which he built on the east bank of the Euphrates near Kūfa to house his family and his guards. Later he transferred the capital to Anbār. It was Manṣūr (754–775), the second 'Abbāsid Caliph and in many ways the founder of the new regime, who established the permanent seat of the 'Abbāsid capital in a new city on the west bank of the Tigris near the ruins of the old Sasanid capital of Ctesiphon, the stones of which were used in building the new city. Its official name was *Madīnat as-Salām*, the city of peace, but it is more frequently known by the name of the Persian village that previously occupied the site—Baghdad. Manṣūr chose the site for good practical reasons. He established the city near a navigable canal linking the Tigris and the Euphrates and occupying a key position on intersecting routes in all directions and on the road to India. In a revealing passage on the foundation of the city the geographer Ya'qūbī tells how Manṣūr halted by the village of Baghdad in the course of a journey and said:

> "This island between the Tigris in the East and the Euphrates in the West is a market place for the world. All the ships that come up the Tigris from Wāsiṭ, Baṣra, Ubulla, Ahwāz, Fars, 'Umān, Yamāma, Baḥrain and beyond will go up and anchor here; wares brought on ships down the Tigris from Mosul, Diyār-Rabī'a, Adharbaijān and Armenia, and along the Euphrates from Diyār-Muḍar, Raqqa, Syria and the border marshes, Egypt and North Africa will be brought and unloaded here. It will be the highway for the people of the Jabal, Iṣfāhān and the districts of Khurāsān. Praise be to God who preserved it for me and caused all those who came before me to neglect it. By God, I shall build it. Then I shall dwell in it as long as I live and my descendants shall dwell in it after me. It will surely be the most flourishing city in the world."

The centre of Baghdad was the round city of some two miles diameter, forming a kind of citadel in which were the Caliph's residence and the quarters of the officials and of the Khurāsānī guards whom the Caliphs had brought with them from the East. Beyond the round city, a great commercial metropolis rapidly developed.

The effects of the transfer were considerable. The centre of gravity had moved from the Mediterranean province of Syria to Mesopotamia, a rich, irrigated river valley and the intersection of many trade-routes. It symbolised the change from a Byzantine succession state to a Middle Eastern Empire of the traditional pattern in which old oriental influences, and notably those of Persia, came to play an ever-increasing part.

The change of dynasty completed a process of development in the organisation of the state which had already begun under the Umayyads. From a tribal Sheikh governing by the unwilling consent of the Arab ruling caste, the Caliph now became an autocrat claiming a divine origin for his authority, resting it on his regular armed forces, and exercising it through a salaried bureaucracy. The increased importance of force as an element of authority is well exemplified in the important position held by the executioner in the 'Abbāsid court, well known to all readers of the *Arabian Nights*. In the new regime pedigree was no help to advancement, but only the favour of the sovereign, and the Arab aristocracy was replaced by an official hierarchy. The new dignity of the Caliph was expressed in new titles. No longer was he the Deputy of the Prophet of God, but simply the Deputy of God, from whom he claimed to derive his authority directly. The same idea is expressed in the resounding title "Shadow of God upon Earth". Whereas the early Caliphs had been Arabs like the rest whom any man could approach and address by name, the 'Abbāsids surrounded themselves with the pomp and ceremonial of an elaborate and hierarchic court and could only be approached through a series of chamberlains. In theory the Caliph was still subject to the rule of the *Sharī'a*, the holy law of Islam. In practice, this check on his authority had limited effect since there was no machinery other than revolt for its enforcement. The 'Abbāsid Caliphate was thus an autocracy based on military force and claiming almost divine right. The 'Abbāsids were stronger than the Umayyads in that they did not depend on the support of the Arabs and could therefore rule rather than persuade. On the other hand, they were weaker than the old oriental despotisms in that they lacked the support of an established feudal caste and of an entrenched priesthood.

'Abbāsid administration was a development of that of the late Umayyads, and Manṣūr openly admitted his great debt to the Umayyad Caliph Hishām in the organisation of the State. But the influence of the old Persian order of the Sasanids became increasingly strong and much 'Abbāsid practice is a deliberate imitation of Sasanid habits which were now becoming known from Persian officials and from surviving Sasanid literature. The 'Abbāsid administration was no longer based on racial discrimination and exclusiveness. Its extensive scribal class was recruited to an increased extent from the Mawālī and enjoyed a high social standing. It was organised in a series of Dīwāns or Ministries, including Dīwāns of Chancery, the Army, the Seal, Finance, Posts and Intelligence, etc. The army of officials employed in these dīwāns were under the supreme control of the Wazīr. This office was an 'Abbāsid innovation, possibly of Persian origin. The Wazīr was the head of the whole administrative machine, and as chief executive under the Caliph exercised immense power. One of the first Wazīrs was a recently Islamised Central Asian called Khālid al-Barmakī, and the office was held by several of the Barmecide family until their overthrow by Hārūn ar-Rashīd in 803.

In the provinces authority was exercised jointly by the Amīr or governor, and the 'Āmil or financial superintendent, with their own staffs and forces and with some measure of autonomy under the general surveillance of the postmaster, whose duty it was to report on events directly to the Dīwān of Posts and Intelligence in Baghdad.

In the Army, the Arab militia was no longer important and the pensions paid to the Arabs were gradually discontinued except for regular serving soldiers. The Army now consisted of paid troops, either full-time regulars or volunteers for a single campaign. The core was the devoted Khurāsānī guards, the mainstay of the new regime. An Arab force known as the *'Arab ad-Dawla*, the Arabs of the Dynasty, was maintained for a while from Arabs loyal to the new regime. It soon lost its importance, however, and in later times the Army came to consist to an increasing extent of specially trained slaves known as *Mamlūks*, most of them of Central Asian Turkish origin.

The 'Abbāsids had come to power on the crest of a religious movement and sought to retain popular support by stressing the religious aspect of their authority. One notices among the early 'Abbāsid Caliphs a persistent courting of the religious leaders and jurisconsults and an insistence, in public at least, on the observance of religious good taste. In the words of a later Arabic historian: "This dynasty ruled the world with a policy of mingled religion and kingship, the best and most religious of men obeyed them out of religion and the remainder obeyed them out of fear." The religious organisation filled the gap left by the break-up of Arab racial unity and served as the cement binding together the diverse ethnic and social elements of the population. The stress on the religious character of society and sovereignty led to frequent accusations of hypocrisy and to the remark of one poet: "Would that the tyranny of the sons of Marwān would return to us, would that the equity of the sons of 'Abbās were in hell!"

It is in the economic life of the 'Abbāsid Empire that we can see most clearly the nature of the changes that the revolution had brought. The Empire disposed of rich resources. Wheat, barley and rice, in that order, were the main crops of the great irrigated river valleys, while dates and olives formed important secondary foods. The Empire was well provided with metals, too. Silver came from the eastern provinces, and especially from the Hindu Kush, where, according to a tenth-century source, ten thousand miners were employed on capitalist lines. Gold was brought from the west, and especially from Nubia and the Sudan, copper from the neighbourhood of Isfāhān, where in the ninth century the copper mines paid a tax of five thousand dirhams; iron from Persia, Central Asia and Sicily Precious stones were found in many parts of the Empire, and pearls were obtained from the rich fisheries of the Persian Gulf. Timber was lacking in the western provinces, but available in some quantity in the east, and an extensive import trade brought supplies from India and beyond.

The 'Abbāsids undertook extensive irrigation works, extending the area of cultivated land and draining swamps, and the historians report a very high yield. The revolution gave the peasants greater possession rights and a more equitable system of tax assessment, based on a percentage of the crop, instead of a fixed rate, as previously. But the status of the peasants was still bad, and in course of time was aggravated by the speculations of wealthy merchants and landowners and by the introduction of slave labour on large estates, which degraded the economic and social standing of free labour.

A mediaeval Muslim encyclopedia divides industry and crafts into two groups—primary, i.e. those supplying the basic needs of mankind; and ancillary, or luxury. The former was divided into food; shelter and clothing. It was the last-named which was by far the most developed in the Islamic Empire. The most important industry, both for the numbers employed and the volume of output, was that of textiles, which began under the Umayyads and was now rapidly expanded. All kinds of goods were produced, both for local consumption and for export—piece-goods, clothes, carpets, tapestries, upholstery, cushions, etc. Linen was made mainly in Egypt where Copts played an important part in the three main centres—Damietta, Tinnīs, and Alexandria. Cotton was originally imported from India, but was soon cultivated in eastern Persia and spread westwards as far as Spain. The manufacture of silk was inherited from the Byzantine and Sasanid Empires and centred in the Persian provinces of Jurjān and Sīstān. Carpets were made almost everywhere, those of Ṭabaristān and Armenia being regarded as the best. The industry was organised partly under state control, partly under private initiative. From late Umayyad times the government had maintained workshops and manufacturing centres for the production of *Ṭirāz*, materials used for the clothing of rulers and for the ceremonial costumes granted as marks of honour to high officials and Army commanders. The usual production system was domestic. The artisans could sell only to state agents or to a private *entrepreneur* who financed them. In some cases the artisans were paid a salary, and in ninth-century Egypt we hear of a rate of half a dirham a day.

Paper was first made in China, according to tradition, in the year 105 B.C. In A.D. 751 the Arabs won a victory over some contingents of a Chinese force east of the Jaxartes. Among their prisoners were some Chinese paper-makers who brought their craft into the world of Islam. Under Hārūn ar-Rashīd paper was introduced to Iraq. Although the use of paper spread rapidly across the Islamic world, reaching Egypt by 800 and Spain by 900, manufacture was at first limited to the eastern provinces where it was first introduced. But from the tenth century onwards there is clear evidence of paper-making in Iraq, Syria, Egypt and even in Arabia, and soon we hear of paper-mills in North Africa and Spain. Known centres include Samarqand, Baghdad, Damascus, Tiberias, Hama, Syrian Tripoli, Cairo, Fez in Morocco and Valencia in Spain.

Other industries include pottery, metalwork, soap and perfumes.

The resources of the Empire, and also the vitally important transit trade between Europe and the Further East, made possible an extensive commercial development, assisted by the establishment of internal order and security and of peaceful relations with neighbouring countries in place of the incessant wars of conquest of the Umayyads.

The trade of the Islamic Empire was of vast extent. From the Persian Gulf ports of Sīrāf, Baṣra and Ubulla and, to a lesser extent, from Aden and the Red Sea ports, Muslim merchants travelled to India, Ceylon, the East Indies and China, bringing silks, spices, aromatics, woods, tin and other commodities, both for home consumption and for re-export. Alternative routes to India and China ran overland through Central Asia. One source lists the goods brought from China as aromatics, silk goods, crockery, paper, ink, peacocks, swift horses, saddles, felt, cinnamon, pure Greek rhubarb; from the

Byzantine Empire as gold and silver utensils, gold coins, drugs, brocades, slave girls, trinkets, locks, hydraulic engineers, agronomes, marble workers and eunuchs, and from India as tigers, panthers, elephants, panther skins, rubies, white sandalwood, ebony and coconuts. From Muslim manuals of navigation that have come down to us it is clear that Muslim navigators were quite at home in eastern seas, where Arab traders were established in China as early as the eighth century.

In Scandinavia, and especially in Sweden, scores of thousands of Muslim coins have been found bearing inscriptions dating from the late seventh to the early eleventh centuries, showing the period of efflorescence of Islamic trade. Many finds of coins along the course of the Volga confirm the evidence of literary sources as to an extensive trade between the Islamic Empire and the Baltic via the Caspian, the Black Sea and Russia. From these countries the Arabs obtained principally furs, skins and amber. The late tenth- century geographer Muqaddasī lists the wares imported through the Volga and Khwārizm as "sable, grey squirrel, ermine, mink, fox, beaver-skins, spotted hare, goat-skins, wax, arrows, birch-bark, fur-caps, fish-glue, fish-teeth, castoreum, amber, shagreen, honey, hazel-nuts, falcons, swords, armour, *khalanj* wood, Slavonic slaves, sheep and cattle." It is unlikely that the Arabs themselves penetrated as far as Scandinavia. More probably they met the northern peoples in Russia, with the Khazars and the Bulgars of the Volga serving as intermediaries. The importance of Arab trade with the north is further shown by the fact that the earliest known Swedish coinage is based on the dirham weight, and by the presence of several Arabic words in old Icelandic literature.

With Africa, too, the Arabs carried on an extensive overland trade, the chief commodities which they imported being gold and slaves. Trade with western Europe was at first broken off by the Arab Conquests, but resumed by the Jews who served as a link between the two hostile worlds. In a frequently quoted passage, the early ninth-century geographer, Ibn Khurradādhbeh, tells of Jewish merchants from the south of France:

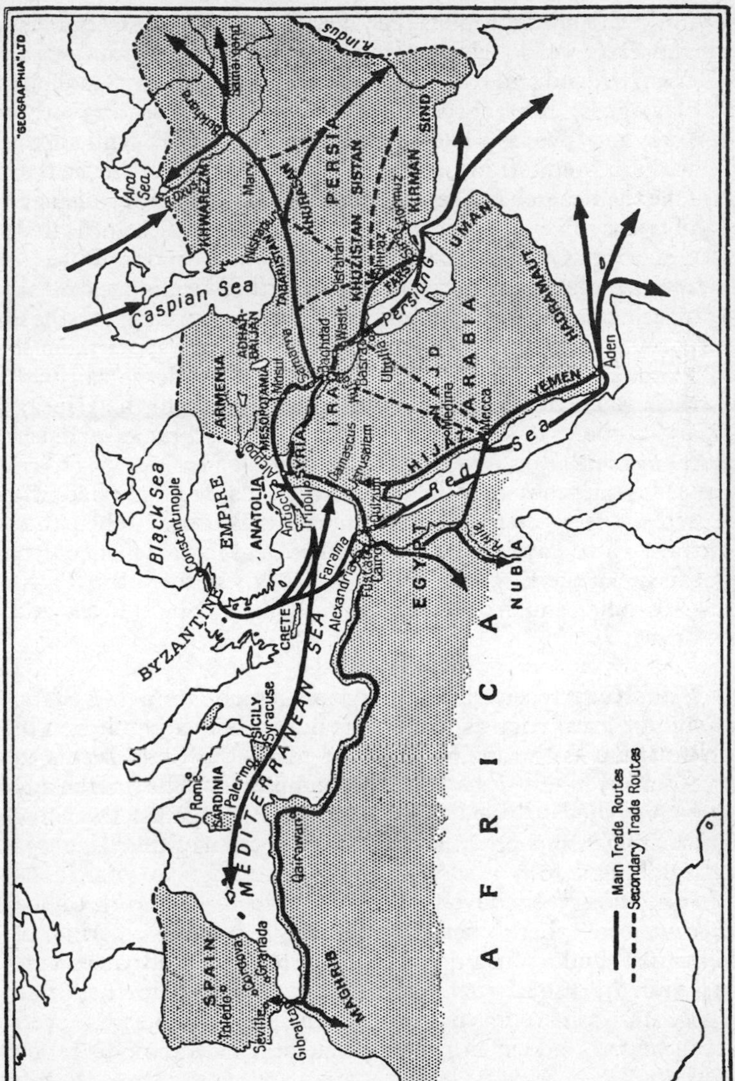

The Islamic Empire—extent and main trade routes

"... who speak Arabic, Persian, Greek, Frankish, Spanish and Slavonic. They travel from west to east and from east to west, by land and by sea. From the west they bring eunuchs, slave-girls, boys, brocade, beaver-skins, sable and other furs, and swords. They take ship from Frank-land in the western Mediterranean sea and land at Faramā, whence they take their merchandise on camel-back to Qulzum, a distance of twenty-five parasangs. Then they sail on the eastern (Red) Sea from Qulzum to Al-Jār and Jedda, and onward to Sind, India and China. From China they bring back musk, aloes, camphor, cinnamon, and other products of those parts, and return to Qulzum. Then they transport them to Faramā and sail again on the western sea. Some sail with their goods to Constantinople, and sell them to the Greeks, and some take them to the king of the Franks and sell them there.

"Sometimes they bring their goods from Frank-land across the western sea and unload at Antioch. Then they travel three days' march overland to Al-Jābiya, whence they sail down the Euphrates to Baghdad, then down the Tigris to Ubulla, and from Ubulla to 'Umān, Sind, India and China. . . ."

If industry received some encouragement from the State, mainly for fiscal reasons, trade was not so helped, and even in such matters as the maintenance of roads the State seems to have done very little to promote commerce. The merchants were compelled to wage a constant struggle against the ever-encroaching bureaucracy. The economic action of the State was at first limited to a general ban on speculation in vital food-stuffs—not very effectively enforced—and to the work of the *Muḥtasib*, an urban official whose task it was to superintend the markets and to ensure good quality material and workmanship and the use of just weights. At a later date the State began to intervene more directly in commerce, even attempting to trade in and monopolise certain commodities for itself.

The growth of large-scale trading and enterprise gave rise

during the ninth century to a development of banking. The economy of the Islamic Empire had been from the first bimetallist, with the Persian silver dirham circulating in the eastern provinces and the Byzantine gold denarius (Arabic, *Dīnār*) in the west. These issues were maintained by the Caliphate with the standard weight of 2·97 grammes for the dirham and of 4·25 grammes for the dīnār. Despite many attempts to stabilise the relative value of these two coins they inevitably fluctuated with the prices of the metals of which they were made, and the *Ṣarrāf*, or money-changer, came to be an essential feature of every Muslim market. In the ninth century he developed into a banker on a large scale, no doubt supported by wealthy traders with money to invest. We hear of banks with a head office in Baghdad and branches in the other cities of the Empire and of an elaborate system of cheques, letters of credit, etc., so developed that it was possible to draw a cheque in Baghdad and cash it in Morocco. In Baṣra, the main centre of the flourishing eastern trade, we are told that every merchant had his bank account and that payments in the bazaar were effected only by cheque and never in cash. In the tenth century we find government banks in the capital with the title of "Bankers of the Presence", who advanced to the government the large sums of ready money required for administrative expenses against a mortgage on uncollected taxes. Owing to the Muslim ban on usury most of the bankers were Jews and Christians.

The flourishing commercial life of the time was reflected in its thought and literature, where we find the upright merchant held up as an ideal ethical type. Traditions attributed to the Prophet include such statements as "In the day of Judgement the honest truthful Muslim merchant will take rank with the martyrs of the faith", "The truthful merchant will sit under the shadow of the throne of God on the Day of Judgement", "Merchants are the couriers of the world and the trusted servants of God upon earth". The Caliph 'Umar I is most improbably quoted as saying, "There is no place where I would be more gladly overtaken by death than in the market place, buying and selling for my family." The essayist Jāḥiẓ in an essay entitled "In praise of merchants and in condemnation of officials" remarks that the approval of God for trading as a way of life is proved by His choice of the trading community of Quraish for His Prophet. The literature of the time includes portraits of the ideal upright merchant and much advice on the investment of money in trade, including such maxims as not to put one's capital into things for which there is a limited demand, such as jewels, which are required only by the wealthy, or learned books, which are required only by scholars, who in any case are few and poor. This particular maxim must have emanated from a writer of theoretical rather than practical experience, since the evidence in general shows that it was precisely the dealers in expensive luxury commodities such as jewels and fine cambric who were the wealthiest and most respected.

All these economic changes brought corresponding social changes and a new set of relationships between the ethnic and social components of the population. The Arab warrior caste was now deposed. It had lost its grants from the treasury and its privileges. From this time onwards the Arab chroniclers speak only rarely of the tribal feuds of the Arabs. This does not mean that they had abated in violence, for as late as the nineteenth century one still finds the descendants of Qais and Kalb at one another's throats in Syria. It does mean that the Arab tribal aristocracy had lost its power to intervene in and influence public affairs and that its feuds and squabbles were no longer of great significance. From this time on the Arab tribesmen began to abandon the Amṣār, some reverting to the nomadism which they had never completely abandoned, others settling on the land. The Islamic town changed in character from the garrison city of an occupying army in a conquered province to a market and exchange, where the merchants and artisans began to organise themselves in guilds for joint aid and defence.

But the Arabs had not entirely lost their supremacy. The government at first was still predominantly Arab in its higher ranks. The dynasty was still Arab and prided itself on its Arabdom, and Arabic was still the sole language of government and culture. The theoretical superiority of the Arabs was maintained and led to the emergence of the Shu'ūbīya movement in literary and intellectual circles, advancing the claims of the non-Arabs to equal standing. But an important change was taking place in the meaning of the word Arab itself. From this time onwards the Arabs ceased to be a closed hereditary caste and became a people, ready to accept, by a sort of naturalisation, any Muslim speaking Arabic as one of themselves. The social emancipation of the Mawālī took the form of their full acceptance as Arabs, and even the Khurāsānī Pretorians of the Caliphs became thoroughly Arabised. The process of Arabisation in the provinces west of Persia was assisted by the scattering of the demobilised Arabs, by the predominance of the Arabic language in the towns and from them in the surrounding countryside. Its development is attested by the first joint Arab-Copt revolt in Egypt in 831. Eventually even the Christians and Jews of Iraq, Syria, Egypt and North Africa began to use Arabic, and the term Arab itself in Arabic usage came to be restricted to the nomads.

In place of the Arab aristocracy the Empire had a new ruling class, the rich and the learned, with the former possessing in many cases enormous fortunes in currency and property. These fortunes were built up by holding government jobs, which were not only highly paid, but offered unlimited opportunities for additional earnings, by trade and banking, by speculation and by the exploitation of the land through ownership or the farming of taxes. An example in one source tells how a young man of an official family invested a fortune of 40,000 dīnārs, which he had inherited. 1,000 went on rebuilding his father's fallen house, 7,000 on furniture, clothes, slave-girls and other amenities; 2,000 he gave to a reliable merchant to trade on his behalf, 10,000 he buried in the ground for emergencies, and with the remaining 20,000 he bought an estate, on the revenues of which he lived.

A word may be said here about the position of the Dhimmis, the non-Muslim subjects of the Empire. The status which they enjoyed has been much idealised by some writers who have magnified the undoubted tolerance of Muslim governments into the granting of complete equality. The Dhimmīs were second-class citizens, paying a higher rate of taxation, suffering from certain social disabilities, and on a few rare occasions subjected to open persecution. But by and large their position was infinitely superior to that of those communities who differed from the established church in western Europe in the same period. They enjoyed the free exercise of their religion, normal property rights, and were very frequently employed in the service of the State, often in the highest offices. They were admitted to the craft guilds, in some of which they actually predominated. They were never called upon to suffer martyrdom or exile for their beliefs.

The first signs of decay in this imposing civilisation were in the structure of political unity. The Empire built by Manṣūr seemed solid enough, despite some rumblings of rebellion, until the reign of Hārūn (786-809), which in many ways marks the apogee of 'Abbāsid power. The early 'Abbāsids had maintained the alliance with the Persian aristocratic wing of the movement that had brought them to power, and the noble Persian house of Barmak, through a dynasty of Wazīrs, had played a central role in the government of the Empire. During the lifetime of Hārūn ar-Rashīd there was a convulsion of obscure origins and circumstances that culminated in the degradation of the house of Barmak and their loss of power, wealth and life itself in what has come to be known in other contexts, too, as a Barmecide feast.

After Hārūn's death, smouldering conflicts burst into open civil war between his sons Amīn and Ma'mūn. Amīn's strength lay mainly in the capital and in Iraq, Ma'mūn's in Persia, and the civil war has been interpreted, on doubtful evidence, as a national conflict between Arabs and Persians, ending in a victory for the latter. It was more probably a continuation of the social struggles of the immediately preceding period, combined with a regional rather than national conflict between Persia and Iraq. Ma'mūn, whose support came mainly from the eastern provinces, for a while projected the transfer of the

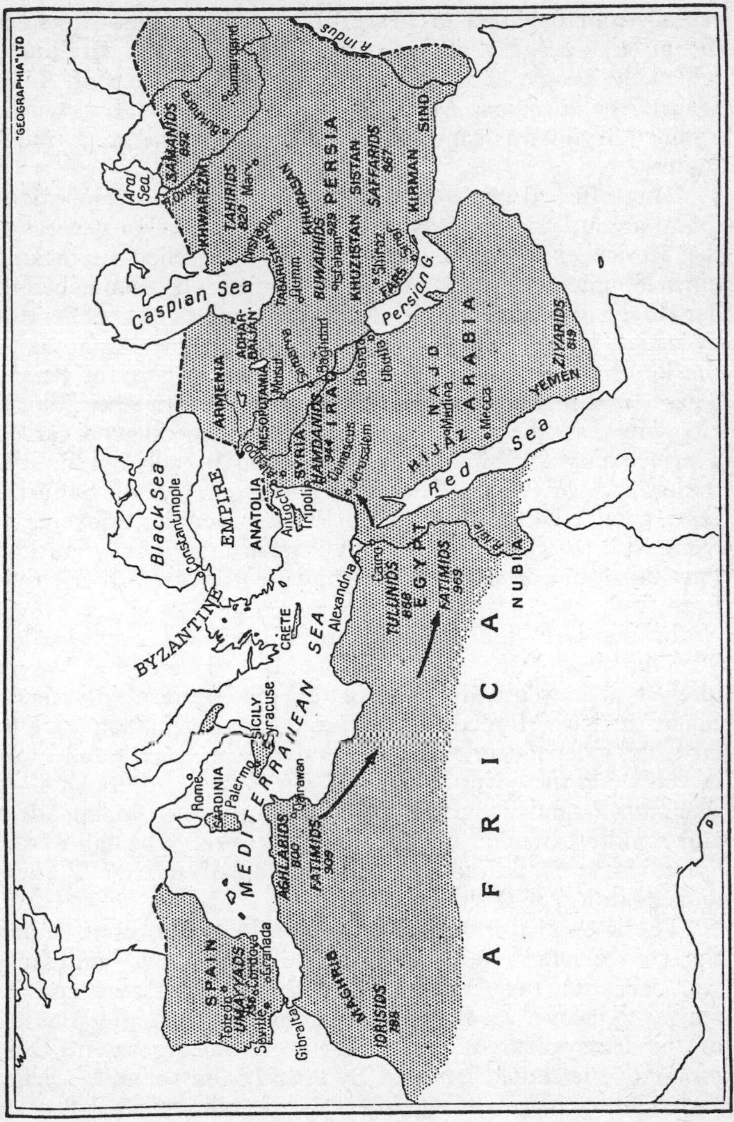

The break-up of political unity in the ninth and tenth centuries

capital from Baghdad to Marv in Khurāsān. This threat to the arterial position of their city and their very livelihood rallied the people of Baghdad in a frenzied defence of Amīn against the invaders. Ma'mūn won the victory, but wisely retained Baghdad as capital and nodal point of the great trade-routes.

Thereafter Persian aristocratic and regional aspirations found an outlet in local dynasties. In 820 a Persian general in the service of Ma'mūn, called Ṭāhir, succeeded in making himself independent in eastern Persia and established a hereditary governorship in his own family. Other Persian dynasties, that of the Ṣaffārids in 867, and the Sāmānids in *ca.* 892, soon established themselves in other parts of Persia. These local regimes were of different character. The Ṭāhirid kingdom was the work of an ambitious general who carved a principality for himself, but remained broadly within the framework of Arabo-Islamic civilisation. The Ṣaffārids represented the upsurge of a Persian popular movement, while with the Sāmānids the old Persian aristocracy returned to political power and the full enjoyment of its former privileges.

In the west the political break-up began even earlier. The removal of the capital eastwards had caused a loss of interest and eventually control in the western provinces. Spain in 756, Morocco in 788, and Tunisia in 800 became virtually independent under local dynasties. Egypt fell away in 868 when the governor Aḥmad ibn Ṭūlūn, a Turkish slave sent from Baghdad, succeeded in making himself independent and rapidly extended his dominion to Syria. The fall of the Ṭūlūnids was followed by the accession of another Turkish dynasty in Egypt of similar origin.

The rise of an independent centre in Egypt, often ruling Syria too, created a new no man's land between Syria and Iraq, and permitted the Arab tribes of the Syrian desert and its fringes to recover the independence they had lost after the fall of the Umayyads. At times they were able to extend their power to the settled lands of Syria and Mesopotamia, seizing and holding cities during intervals of military weakness or disunity and establishing shortlived but brilliant Bedouin dynasties like that of the Ḥamdānids of Mosul and Aleppo in the tenth century. Soon the Caliph retained direct control only of Iraq, and for the rest of the Empire had to be content with occasional tribute and nominal recognition by local hereditary dynasties in the form of a mention in the Friday prayer in the mosque and in the inscriptions on the coinage.

As long as Baghdad retained control of the vital trade-routes leading through it the political break-up did not impede, but seems in some ways actually to have helped the expansion of economic and cultural life. But soon more dangerous developments appeared and the authority of the Caliph dwindled even in the capital itself. The excessive luxury of the Court and the overweight of the bureaucracy produced financial disorder and a shortage of money, later aggravated by the drying up or loss to invaders of sources of precious metal.

The Caliphs found a remedy in the farming out of state revenues, eventually with local governors as tax farmers. Their duties were to remit an agreed sum to the central government and to maintain local forces and officials. These farmer-governors soon became the real rulers of the Empire and were rapidly identified with the Army commanders. From the time of Mu'tasim (833–842) and Wāthiq (842–847), the Caliphs gradually lost control to their own army commanders and guards, who were often able to appoint and depose them at will. These commanders and guards consisted to an increasing extent of Turkish Mamlūks. In the year 935 the office of *Amīr al-Umarā*, or commander of commanders, was created in order to indicate the primacy of the commander in the capital over the rest. Finally, in 945, the Persian house of Buwaih, which had already established itself as a virtually independent dynasty in western Iran, invaded the capital and destroyed the last shreds of the Caliph's independence. From this time onwards, with rare intervals, the Caliphs were at the mercy of a series of mayors of the palace, most of them Persian or Turkish, ruling through the armed forces under their own command. Although he retained the status and dignity of the office of supreme sovereign of Islam, head of both Church and State, or rather of the intermingled organism of the two, the Caliph's real power had gone, and his investiture of a commander or governor was merely a formal *post facto* recognition of an existing situation.

VI

"THE REVOLT OF ISLAM"

"Et une heure, je suis descendu dans le mouvement d'un boulevard de Bagdad où des compagnies ont chanté la joie du travail nouveau. . . ."

(Rimbaud, *Les Illuminations*)

THE rapid economic development of the Near and Middle East in the centuries that followed the accession of the 'Abbāsid Caliphs subjected the social fabric of the Empire to a series of dangerous stresses and strains, generating numerous movements of discontent and open rebellion against the established order. These movements were mainly economic and social in origin, some with a national colouring. Diverse in their causes and circumstances and in the composition of their following, they have this much in common, that they were almost all religiously expressed. Whenever a grievance or a conflict of interests created a faction in Islam, its doctrines were a theology, its instrument a sect, its agent a missionary, its leader usually a Messiah or his representative. But to describe these socially motivated religious heresies as "cloaks" or "masks", behind which scheming men hid their real and material purposes in order to deceive the pious, is to distort history. The Islamic State, born of Muḥammad's community in Medina and fostered by the ancient divine monarchies of the Orient, was in theory and in the popular conception a theocracy, in which God was the sole source of both power and law and the sovereign His vicegerent on earth. The faith was the official credo of the established order, the cult the external and visible symbol of its identity and cohesion, conformity to them, however perfunctory, the token and pledge of loyalty. Orthodoxy meant the acceptance of the existing order, heresy or apostasy its criticism or rejection.

In a society so constituted, where both in the structure of

government and in the minds and feelings of men Church and State were indistinguishably fused, religion and religious controversy played the part that politics play in the modern world, and almost every movement, whatever its motivation, sought in religion not a mask, but the necessary and organic expression in public and social terms of the ambitions and discontents that drove it. There were, of course, exceptions—palace *coups d'état* and military *émeutes* in times of political weakness, peasant revolts and city riots in times of economic strain. But these movements were sporadic and for the most part unorganised, restricted to the time, place and circumstances of their immediate origin, often of purely personal significance. Whenever a group of men sought to offer an organised and sustained challenge to the social order they found expression in a religious sect as naturally and inevitably as their modern counterparts in a political party.

The 'Abbāsid Caliphate had to face threats of this kind from its very inception. In 752 a rising in Syria took place in support of the claims of the deposed Umayyad dynasty to which that province for long retained its loyalty. Soon even this movement fell in with the general trend of development, and the pro-Umayyad party began to speak of a Messianic figure of the Umayyad House who would in course of time return to this world and establish a reign of justice. The Shī'a, too, soon showed their disappointment with the new regime which they themselves had helped to establish. A pretender of the line of 'Alī, known as "Muḥammad of the Pure Soul", organised a conspiracy and attempted to proclaim himself as Mahdī in Jerusalem. Failing in Palestine, he repeated his attempt in Medina, but was defeated and killed in 762.

Far more important was a series of movements in Persia connected in their origins with the sect from which the 'Abbāsids themselves had emerged. The 'Abbāsid revolution was brought about by an alliance of elements opposed to the Umayyads, including Muslim dissidents, both Persian and Arab, and Persians of both aristocratic and humble status. After the success of the revolution the alliance broke up and its component elements reverted to their former state of conflict, aggravated by frustration and disappointment. Abū Muslim, the popular leader who more than any other single individual was the architect of 'Abbāsid victory, was put to death by the second 'Abbāsid Caliph, Al-Manṣūr. Other leaders of the sect received similar treatment. The Caliphs continued to rely on Persian and especially Khurāsānian support, but in place of Abū Muslim and his like came the aristocratic house of the Barmecides, who for several reigns played a dominant role in the life of the capital and assured to the government the support of the old Persian ruling circles.

The resentments of the subject population found expression in a series of religious movements in different parts of Persia, with predominantly peasant support. These movements were to some extent national in that the regime that they opposed was still regarded by them as Arab and in that the religious background of their ideology was Iranian. But their doctrines were not Zoroastrian. The orthodox followers of the old State religion of Iran, the members of the aristocratic ruling caste, were for the time being identified with the regime, and it was not until the reign of Ma'mūn that the princes of Persia created their own movements towards independence by establishing autonomous principalities in the eastern provinces. The religious inspiration of these rebels came rather from the old Iranian heresies, which in pre-Islamic times were linked with the revolt of the lower and middle classes against the Sasanid monarchy. The most important of these was Mazdak, a communist revolutionary who in the sixth century had almost overthrown the Sasanid Empire. Although the movement of Mazdak had been crushed in blood by the Sasanid Emperor Chosroes Anushirvan, its memory lingered on among the peasant population and its doctrines played a vital part in the formation of religious movements which began in late Umayyad times and continued under the early 'Abbāsids. The memory of Abū Muslim himself was also frequently invoked by Persian rebels who claimed to be his heirs and avengers against the Caliphs who had betrayed him. At first these movements were Iranian in their beliefs; later they became syncretist, preaching a mingling of Mazdakite and extremist Shī'ite ideas. The orthodox Zoroastrians remained aloof or actively hostile.

The first whose name is recorded was Bihāfarīd, a former Zoroastrian, who appeared in Nīshāpūr around the year 749, claiming to be a Prophet. Little is known of his earlier life, except that he had spent some years in China, possibly for trade. The main opposition to him came not from the Muslims, who regarded his movement with indifference, but from the orthodox Zoroastrians, and especially the priesthood, who appealed to the 'Abbāsids for support against him and were largely responsible for his defeat within two years.

The death of Abū Muslim brought a change. The more extreme among his followers staged a series of peasant revolts, usually claiming that he was not really dead, but in hiding, and would return to his people. In 755 Sonpādh, a former associate of Abū Muslim and probably a Mazdakī, rose in revolt. He seems to have come from a village near Nīshāpūr. He rapidly won considerable support among the peasantry of western Persia, including both Zoroastrian and Muslim heretics. His movement spread rapidly and his followers captured several towns. The Arabic sources put their numbers at between 90,000–100,000. They were soon defeated by an army sent by Manṣūr. Two years later a parallel revolt was led by another former agent of Abū Muslim, known as Iṣḥāq the Turk, because he had been sent to preach the faith among the Central Asian Turks. He, too, was crushed. In 767, Ustādhsīs led a revolt in Khurāsān, which for a while gravely threatened the security of the Empire.

Far more dangerous than any other of these was the revolt of Muqanna' (the Veiled One), who, incidentally, forms the subject of an episode in Moore's *Lalla Rukh*. He was so called because of his habit of wearing a veil over his face in order to conceal, according to his followers, its radiance, according to his opponents, its deformities. Muqanna' was a Persian heretic and a laundryman by profession. He began his preaching in Merv and his movement rapidly spread all over Khurāsān and into Central Asia, where Bokhara was for a while its stronghold. Here, too, one sees signs of a connection both with Mazdak and with Abū Muslim, and the orthodox sources do not fail to accuse him of preaching and practising communism of both property and women. His movement lasted longer than those of his predecessors and was able to survive from 776 to 789.

By far the most serious of these movements was that of Bābak (816–837), which was distinguished at once by its extent, its duration, its leadership and its cohesion. Bābak was a heretic and a man of remarkable military and political gifts. His sect, the Khurramīya, are said to have been mainly villagers; his contemporary Māzyār, another Khurramī rebel, "ordered the peasants . . . to attack the landowners and plunder their possessions". There is some evidence of support also from the Dihqāns, the Persian squirearchy, many of whom had degenerated by this time into little more than ordinary peasants, with a proud recollection of nobility. The centre of the movement was in Adharbaijān, of which the geographer Yāqūt remarks, somewhat acidly, that it had always been a centre of sedition and strife. From Adharbaijān it spread to south-west Persia, where Kurdish as well as Persian elements rallied to it, to the Caspian provinces of the north, and westwards into Armenia. At one stage Bābak seems to have had a working alliance with the Byzantine Emperor against the common foe. His position astride the northern trade-routes made him a really dangerous enemy. For seven years his arms were completely successful, defeating four of the Caliph Ma'mūn's generals, but after the accession of Mu'taṣim in 833 the general improvement in the security of the Empire permitted a more determined military effort which restricted the Bābakīs to Adharbaijān and eventually crushed them.

Of quite a different character was the revolt of the negro slaves known as Zanj, between 869 and 883. Islam was a slave-holding society and in some areas still is. But slaves were not, as in the Roman Empire, the main basis of production, which depended rather on free or semi-free peasants and artisans. The slaves were mainly employed for domestic or military use, the latter known as Mamlūks and forming in effect a privileged military caste which in time came to exercise a dominating influence on the affairs of the State. There were, however, exceptions. Slaves were employed for manual labour on a number of large-scale enterprises: in mines, in the fleets, in the drainage of marshes, etc. The growth of a class of large capitalists and *entrepreneurs* with considerable liquid capital at their disposal led to the purchase and employment of slaves in large numbers for agricultural use. They were herded together in settlements, often thousands belonging to a single landowner or *entrepreneur*. Slaves of this kind were mainly negro, obtained more especially from East Africa by capture, purchase, or in the form of tribute from subordinate states.

Such were the slaves of the salt flats east of Baṣra, where unprecedented numbers were employed by the wealthy men of that city in draining the salt marshes in order to prepare the ground for agriculture and to extract the salt for sale. They worked in gangs of from five hundred to five thousand; one gang of fifteen thousand is mentioned. Their conditions were extremely bad. Their labour was hard and exacting and they received only a bare and inadequate keep consisting, according to the Arabic sources, of flour, semolina and dates. Many of them were Africans of recent arrival with little or no Arabic, and we are told that their leader had to employ interpreters in order to address them. He was a Persian known as 'Alī ibn Muḥammad, who claimed 'Alid ancestry and may perhaps have been of Arab descent. After a number of unsuccessful attempts at sedition in various places, including Baṣra, where he narrowly escaped capture and imprisonment, he went to the saltpetre area in September 869, and began to work on the slaves. He reminded them, says the Arabic historian Ṭabarī, of the evil state in which they lived and claimed that "God would save them from it through him and that he desired to raise their status and make them masters of slaves and wealth and dwellings". The last words reveal a weakness of the movement—it had no real programme of reform, no general aim of abolishing slavery, but was rather a revolt of specific slaves to better their own position. 'Alī fulfilled his promise when the victories that he won enabled him to give captured Muslims as slaves to his followers.

Even this semi-barbaric movement was sufficiently affected by the prevailing tone of Islamic society to seek religious expression. Though the leader of the Zanj claimed 'Alid descent he did not join the Shī'a, but rather the sect of the Khawārij, the equalitarian anarchists who had proclaimed in earlier times that the best man should be Caliph though he be an Abyssinian slave. In accordance with Khārijite doctrines the Zanj regarded all other Muslims as infidels, subject to slavery or the sword when captured.

The movement spread very rapidly and was joined by one gang after another and later probably also by runaway slaves from the towns and villages. The black troops of the Imperial armies sent against them deserted to them, enriching them with arms and trained manpower, while the prospect of booty brought them the support of the neighbouring Bedouin tribes and of the marsh Arabs. Some free peasants of the area are said to have rallied to the Zanj leader and helped him with supplies. There is little sign of support from discontented free elements in the towns, though the sources tell us that two of 'Alī's lieutenants were a miller and a lemonade seller.

The military record of the Zanj was brilliant. One Imperial army after another suffered defeat, enriching them with slaves, booty, and especially arms. In October, 869, they attacked Baṣra, but failed to capture the city. A counter-offensive by the Baṣrans was defeated, however, and shortly after the Zanj built themselves a new capital city known as Al-Mukhtāra, "The Chosen", on a dry spot on the salt flats. We have, unfortunately, no information as to their system of government. On the 19th June, 870, the Zanj captured and sacked the flourishing commercial seaport of Ubulla, greatly strengthening their forces with liberated slaves. Shortly after they expanded into south-west Persia, capturing the city of Ahwāz.

The movement was by now a major threat to the Empire. It dominated important areas of southern Iraq and south-west Persia, had captured several cities, was pressing hard on Baṣra, the second city of the central provinces, and lay across the south-eastern lines of communication of the capital itself. On the 7th September, 871, they captured and sacked Basra itself, but wisely evacuated it immediately after. Meanwhile they had defeated several more Imperial forces, and in 878 captured the old garrison city of Wāsiṭ. By the following year they were raiding within seventeen miles of Baghdad. This marked the peak point of their achievement. The active and energetic regent Muwaffaq, brother of the reigning Caliph, now began to organise at tremendous cost a major expeditionary force. By February, 881, he had expelled the Zanj from all their conquests and confined them to their capital of Al-Mukhtāra. The leader refused the tempting offer of a free pardon and a state pension, and after a long siege the city succumbed to assault on 11th August, 883. The head of ʿAlī was brought to Baghdad on a pole in November.

These movements of peasant revolt in Persia and the slave revolt of southern Iraq seem to have left no permanent mark on the course of Islamic history and wrought no radical change in the structure of Islamic society. They left behind them only an undercurrent of discontent and dissension which found periodic expression in a series of abortive movements; but the growing discontent of the common people of the Empire was to find expression in another movement far more significant and far more lasting in its effects. This was the Ismāʿīlī movement, an offshoot of the Shīʿa. We have seen how Shīʿism developed in its early days from an Arab party to a Muslim sect, and achieved a first resounding success in the accession of the ʿAbbāsids. This victory ended the importance of the line of Shīʿite pretenders descended from Muḥammad ibn al-Ḥanafīya. Henceforth the leaders of the Shīʿa are of the Fāṭimid line, the descendants of ʿAlī by his wife Fāṭima, the daughter of the Prophet. The *Imāms*, as these Shī'ite pretenders were known to their followers, were in their eyes the sole rightful Caliphs. But the powers they claimed were far greater than those of the ʿAbbāsids. The Shīʿite *Imām* was a divinely inspired religious pontiff, claiming infallibility and demanding unquestioning obedience.

On the death of the Imām Jaʿfar in 765, his followers split into two groups, supporting the claims to succession of his sons Mūsā and Ismāʿīl. The followers of the former recognised the descendants of Mūsā until the 12th Imām after 'Alī. He disappeared in obscure circumstances and his return is awaited by the so-called Twelver Shī'a to this day. The Twelver Shī'a were generally moderate in their doctrines, which differed to no great extent from those of Sunnī Islam. A French scholar has described them, with more felicity than accuracy, as "His Majesty's Opposition" to the 'Abbāsid Caliphs.

Far different was the evolution of the Ismā'īlī group, which inherited the extremist and revolutionary character of the earlier movement. The eighth and early ninth centuries may be described as a period of revolutionary incubation, during which Ismā'īl, his son Muḥammad, and a number of devoted followers organised the structure and propaganda of the sect. Its doctrines differ markedly from those of orthodox Islam, including many neo-Platonic and Indian ideas. These were introduced by the doctrine of esoteric interpretation according to which every verse in the Qur'ān had two meanings, the one exoteric and literal, the other esoteric and known only to the initiate. The secret doctrines of the sect were disseminated through a kind of masonic hierarchy of grades of initiation, in the highest of which the complete system was revealed to the convert. This secret organisation helped the sect to survive and flourish despite the vigilance of the 'Abbāsid police. The titular head of the sect was the Imām, an infallible religious leader of the line of 'Alī through Ismā'īl. In certain circumstances the Imām might delegate his powers to another person by a kind of spiritual affiliation. The latter then became a trustee or delegate Imām with many, though not all, of the powers of his master.

At the beginning of the tenth century the social crisis of the Empire was reaching breaking point. The defeated peasants and slaves still nourished their resentments, while the growing concentration of capital and labour had created a large, discontented town proletariat. In 920–921, the financial operations of the Wazīr led to bread riots in the capital and to simmering discontent all over the Empire. The attitude of the dispossessed to orthodox religion is well expressed in some verses of a poet of the period:

"By God, I shall not pray to God while I am bankrupt,
Let the Shaikh al-Jalīl and Fā'iq pray to Him . . .
Why should I pray—where are my wealth, my mansion,
And where my horses, trappings, golden belts?
Were I to pray, when I do not own
An inch of earth, then I would be a hypocrite."

For all these elements the doctrines of the Ismā'īlī propagandists had a ready appeal. The Ismā'īlīs themselves do not throw much light in their writings on the social doctrines of the sect, but from the refutations of the orthodox theologians it is clear that the threat which they offered to the existing order was regarded as primarily social rather than religious. The theologian Al-Baghdādī (translated by A. S. Halkin) quotes an alleged Ismā'īlī document as saying:

> "The true aspect of this is simply that their master (Muḥammad) forbade to them the enjoyment of the good and inspired their hearts with fear of a hidden Being who cannot be apprehended. This is the God in whose existence they believe. He related traditions to them about the existence of what they will never witness, such as resurrection from the graves, retribution, paradise and hell. Thus he soon subjugated them and reduced them to slavery to himself during his lifetime and to his offspring after his death. In this way he arrogated to himself the right to enjoy their wealth, for he says: 'I ask you no reward for it except friendliness to my relatives' (Qur'ān, lxiii, 23). His dealings with them were on a cash basis, but their dealings with him were on credit. He required of them an immediate exchange of their lives and property for a future promise which would never be realised."

Although the document is probably not genuine, it is still valuable as showing how the threat was understood. Ghazālī, one of the major theologians of Islam, observes repeatedly in his refutation of the "abominations of the Ismā'īlīs" that the main danger of the sect was its appeal to the common people.

At first these sects seem to have been active mainly in rural and tribal areas. Soon, however, they acquired a considerable following among the town populations. The Ismā'īlīs may have created, and certainly used, the Islamic guilds as instruments in their organisation, and for centuries afterwards the catechisms and structure of the guilds show many traces of Ismā'īlī influence. A charge frequently brought against the Ismā'īlīs and similar sects by their orthodox opponents was that they practised communism of property and women. An Arabic source preserves an interesting account of the activities of a missionary in the neighbourhood of Kūfa about the middle of the ninth century. Having converted the inhabitants of some villages to his doctrine, we are told, he imposed on them an ever-increasing series of taxes and levies and finally

> "the duty of *Ulfa* (union). This duty consisted of assembling all their goods in one place and enjoying them in common without any one retaining any personal property which might give him an advantage over the others. . . . He assured them that they did not need to keep any property because all the land belonged to them and to no one else. 'That,' he told them, 'is the test by which you are proved so that we may know how you will behave.' He urged them to buy and prepare arms. . . . The missionaries appointed in each village a trustworthy man to assemble all that the people of the village owned by way of cattle, sheep, jewellery, provisions, etc. He clothed the naked and met all their needs, leaving no poor man among them, nor any needy and infirm. Every man worked with diligence and emulation at his task in order to deserve high rank by the benefit he brought. The woman brought what she earned by weaving, the child brought his wages for scaring away birds. Nobody among them owned anything beyond his sword and his arms. When he had established all this and when every one had agreed to conform to it, he ordered the

> missionaries to assemble all the women on a certain night so that they might mix indiscriminately with all the men. This, he said, was true mutual friendship and brotherhood."

There is no evidence in the Ismā'īlī sources of any such practices, and it seems likely that the charge of communism is a reflection of the social aspirations of the Ismā'īlīs, that of libertinism of the higher status that they accorded to women.

The movement came into the open in the early years of the tenth century. Between 901 and 906 armed bands of a related group known as the Carmathians ravaged Syria, Palestine and northern Mesopotamia. The sources preserve the text of a sermon preached in Ḥims during its occupation by them: "O God, guide us with the Caliph, the heir, the Awaited One, the Mahdī, the Master of the Time, the Commander of the Faithful, the Mahdī. O God, fill the earth with justice and equity and destroy his enemies. O God, destroy his enemies."

Far more important was the Carmathian movement in the province of Baḥrain (now called Al-Hasa), on the gulf coast of Arabia. The soil was fertile for revolutionary movements. The province was isolated and difficult of access, with a mixed population and many survivors of the Zanj revolt. Some time at the beginning of the tenth century Carmathian missionaries became the dominant power in the province, expelling the representatives of the central government. Unfortunately, very little information has come down to us on the regime which they established. Our knowledge comes primarily from the writings of two travellers, both pro-Ismā'īlī, who visited the area. The first, who went there in the latter half of the tenth century, describes the Carmathian state as a sort of oligarchic republic. The ruler was a first among equals, governing with the aid of a committee of his close associates. This account is confirmed by the narrative of a Persian Ismā'īlī who visited Baḥrain some time in the eleventh century. He found the Carmathian republic still flourishing. There were, he says, more than 20,000 inhabitants capable of bearing arms in the capital, Laḥsā. They were governed by a council of six, who ruled with equity and justice and who, when they gave audience, spoke in tones of softness and modesty. They observed neither fasts nor prayers, and the only mosque was one built at private cost for orthodox pilgrims. There were no taxes or tithes (the earlier traveller speaks of many). The council owned 30,000 negro slaves who did agricultural labour. If any one was impoverished or indebted, he was re-established with the aid of others. Any foreign artisan coming to Laḥsā was given on arrival sufficient money to establish himself. Repairs for poor house-owners were executed at public cost and corn was ground free of charge in State mills. Commercial transactions were carried on with token money which was not exportable. The two travellers' description of the regime is confirmed on one point by Carmathian coins which have been found, struck in the name of the Committee.

Another area of Ismā'īlī success was the Yemen, where in 901 a missionary established himself and rapidly won power. From the Yemen he sent envoys to India and to North Africa and probably to other areas also. The North African mission achieved brilliant success in Tunisia, and in 908 was able to enthrone the Imām 'Ubaidallah as the first Fāṭimid Caliph. The Fāṭimids had thus in several respects followed the tactics of the 'Abbāsids themselves in their accession to power. They had made use of the secretly organised propaganda of a heterodox sect, and had made their decisive attempt to win power in one of the remoter provinces of the Empire. They diverged from the 'Abbāsids in two important respects, probably related to one another. Unlike the 'Abbāsids, they failed to assume universal control of the world of Islam. Unlike them, too, they remained the heads of the sect which had brought them to power.

The first three Fāṭimid Caliphs reigned only in North Africa, where they encountered a number of difficulties. The establishment of a state and a dynasty involved different requirements from those of a revolutionary opposition sect. At the very beginning intransigents were not wanting who accused the new Caliphs of watering down and betraying the tenets of

Ismā'īlism. At a later date the Fāṭimids were to come into conflict with the Carmathians of Baḥrain for much the same reasons. The expansion of the new dynasty eastwards was accomplished after three unsuccessful attempts by Mu'izz, the fourth Caliph, who conquered Egypt in 969. The conquest had been long prepared by secret emissaries and propagandists, who had undermined the resistance of the Egyptians. The conquest of Egypt was followed almost immediately by a clash with the Carmathians, who, for the moment, constituted a real danger to the new regime. Later they seemed to have returned to their Fāṭimid allegiance.

Mu'izz was well served by two remarkable men. One was his general Jawhar, a Mamlūk of European origin who was the real conqueror of Egypt. It was he who built the new city of Cairo as Fāṭimid capital, and the great mosque of Al-Azhar as the centre of their faith. Converted to orthodoxy centuries later, the Azhar Mosque has remained to the present day one of the main centres of Islamic thought and religious life. The other great servant of Mu'izz was Ya'qūb ibn Killis, an Islamised Jew of Baghdadi origin who had joined Mu'izz in Tunisia and helped him before, during and after the conquest. Ya'qūb ibn Killis was a financial genius, who organised the taxation and civil service system which lasted almost throughout the period of Fāṭimid rule.

The Fāṭimids rapidly extended their sway into Palestine, Syria, and Arabia, and for a while greatly surpassed the power and influence of the orthodox Caliphs in Baghdad. The peak of the Fāṭimid period in Egypt was the reign of the Caliph Mustanṣir (1036–1094), under whom the Fāṭimid Empire included the whole of North Africa, Sicily, Egypt, Syria and western Arabia. In 1056–57 a pro-Fāṭimid general succeeded in seizing even Baghdad itself and in proclaiming the sovereignty of the Fāṭimid Caliph from the pulpits of the 'Abbāsid capital. He was driven out in the following year, however, and thereafter the power of the Fāṭimids declined. The breakdown was first noticeable in the civil administration, and led to the rise of a series of military autocrats who exercised their authority in Cairo just as their counterparts had already been doing in Baghdad for some time. Deprived of their immense powers, and reduced to the status of helpless puppets of the Amīrs, the Caliphs gradually lost the support of the sectaries and their regime was finally abolished by Saladin, who restored Egypt to orthodoxy.

The regime of the Fāṭimids in Egypt at its height differs in a number of respects from those that had preceded it. At the top was the infallible Imām, an absolute monarch, ruling by hereditary right transmitted by the divine will through a divinely ordained family. His government was centralised and hierarchic and was divided into three branches: religious, military and bureaucratic. The last two were in charge of the Wazīr, a civilian, under the Caliph. The religious branch consisted of a hierarchy of missionaries in several grades under a missionary-in-chief, who was an extremely influential political personage. This department was responsible for the higher schools of learning and for the propagandist organisation of the Ismā'īlī sect and seems to have played a role not unlike that of the Party in modern one-party dictatorships. The propagandist branch directed a vast army of agents throughout the eastern provinces still under the nominal control of the 'Abbāsid Caliph in Baghdad. The effectiveness of this propaganda can be seen in a number of ways. From Iraq to the borders of India repeated outbreaks attested the activity of the Ismā'īlī agents, while the intellectual life of the whole of Islam testifies in a number of ways to the seductive appeal of the Ismā'īlī allegiance for the radical intelligentsia. The poets Mutanabbī (*d.* 965) and Abu'l-'Alā al-Ma'arrī (*d.* 1057), two of the greatest in Arabic literature, were both strongly influenced by Ismā'īlī ideas. In Iraq an encyclopaedist movement was organised by a group known as "The Sincere Brethren of Baṣra". These published a series of fifty-one epistles covering all branches of knowledge known at that time, and with a strong Ismā'īlī bias. The Epistles of the Sincere Brethren were read from India to Spain and exercised a vast influence on later writers. Their spread was helped by the organisation of semi-secret study groups under the direction of members of the Brotherhood.

The Fāṭimid period was also an epoch of great commercial and industrial efflorescence. Except for a few periods of famine due to the misbehaviour of the Nile or of military cliques the era was one of great prosperity. From the first, Fāṭimid governments realised the importance of trade both for the prosperity of their Empire and for the extension of its influence. Ya'qūb ibn Killis initiated a commercial drive which later rulers followed. The pre-Fāṭimid trade of Egypt had been meagre and limited. The Fāṭimids developed plantations and industries in Egypt and began an important export trade of Egyptian products. In addition they developed a wide net of commercial relations, especially with Europe and with India. In the West they established close relations, dating back to their early Tunisian days, with the Italian city republics, more particularly with Amalfi, Pisa and Venice. A great volume of seaborne trade passed between Egypt and the West, and Egyptian ships and merchants sailed as far as Spain. The two main harbours under Fāṭimid rule were Alexandria and Syrian Tripoli, both markets of world-wide importance. The Fāṭimid fleets controlled the eastern Mediterranean.

In the East the Fāṭimids developed important contacts with India, gradually extending their sovereignty southward over both shores of the Red Sea. They succeeded in shifting the Indian trade of the Middle East from the Persian Gulf to the Red Sea and especially to the great Fāṭimid port of 'Aidhāb on the Sudanese coast. They traded too with Byzantium and with the Muslim States, though these were of less importance. Wherever the Egyptian merchant went, the Ismā'īlī missionary was not far behind, and soon we find the same ferment of ideas among the Muslims both of Spain and of India.

With the decline of the Fāṭimid Caliphate at home, the links between the dynasty and the sect grew weaker and were eventually broken. The Fāṭimid Caliphate lingered on for a while as a puppet dynasty in Egypt and was eventually abolished, but in the eastern lands of the Caliphate, now under the rule of the Turkish Seljuqs, the revolutionary organisation took on a new lease of life.

VII

THE ARABS IN EUROPE

"Que Castillos son aquellos? Altos son y reluzian!
—El Alhambra era, señor, y la otra la mezquita."
(*Romance de Abenamar*)

THE Arabs in pre-Islamic times were not entirely unacquainted with the sea. For centuries before the rise of Islam the peoples of southern Arabia built ships and carried on important maritime traffic in the Red Sea and Indian Ocean. But the northern Arabs, and particularly those of the Ḥijāz and of the Syrian and Iraqi borderlands, were primarily a continental people, with little knowledge of the sea or of navigation. It is one of the most striking features of the great Islamic conquests that they should have adapted themselves so readily to this new form of activity. Within a few years of their occupation of the Syrian and Egyptian coastlines the people of the landlocked deserts of Arabia had built and manned great war fleets which were able to meet and defeat the powerful and experienced Byzantine navies and to give to the Caliphate that vital prerequisite of its safety and expansion—the naval control of the Mediterranean.

The conquest of Syria and Egypt brought a long stretch of Mediterranean coastline under Arab control, with many ports and a seafaring population. The Arabs, who had hitherto met only Byzantine armies, now met Byzantine navies too, and the brief Byzantine reoccupation of Alexandria from the sea in 645 offered them an early warning of the significance of sea power. They were quick to react. The credit for the creation of the Muslim navies belongs primarily to two men, the Caliph Mu'āwiya and the Governor of Egypt, 'Abdallah ibn Sa'd ibn Abī Sarḥ. Both in Alexandria and in the ports of the Syrian littoral the Muslims equipped and manned war fleets which soon won victories as striking as those of the Muslim armies.

The first great naval battle occurred in 655, when a Muslim fleet of two hundred ships inflicted a crushing defeat on a larger Byzantine fleet off the Anatolian coast.

When the 'Abbāsids transferred the seat of the Caliphate from Syria to Baghdad the interest of the central government in the Mediterranean decreased, but the independent Muslim rulers of Egypt and North Africa long maintained fleets that dominated the Middle Sea from end to end. The Fāṭimid Caliphs of Egypt, we are told, had at one time no fewer than five thousand sea captains sailing under their orders. During the ninth century an increasing volume of Muslim merchant shipping linked the ports of the Muslim coasts of the Mediterranean with one another and with the Christian ports of the north.

The first warlike activities of the newly formed Muslim fleets were directed against the Byzantine islands of Cyprus, Crete and Rhodes, which were among the main bases of the Byzantine navies in the eastern Mediterranean. The Arab historians tell us that the first Caliphs were unwilling to authorise expeditions across the sea, and 'Umar is quoted as forbidding his generals to advance to any place "which I cannot reach on my camel". In 649, the Caliph 'Uthmān, somewhat unwillingly, permitted Mu'āwiya to carry out a first raid on Cyprus. This was followed by brief occupations of both Rhodes and Crete, and during the Umayyad period the Arabs were able to hold for a while the peninsula of Cyzicus in the Sea of Marmara itself and to use it as the naval base of a combined sea and land attack on the Imperial City of Constantinople.

The occupation of the eastern islands was for the most part brief and transitory. Far more significant was the Arab attack on Sicily. The first raids on this island resulted from the initiative of Mu'āwiya and came from the Near East and Libya. Later raids came from Tunisia rather than from the Orient and were helped by the occupation of the island of Pantellaria, *ca.* 700. The first definite attempts at conquest did not come till 740 when Ḥabīb ibn Abī 'Ubaida besieged Syracuse and extracted tribute, but was forced to abandon the attempt and return home to meet a Berber revolt in Africa. After another raid in 752–3 a period of uneasy peace followed, during which a number of truces were signed between the Byzantine authorities on the island and the now independent Muslim rulers in Tunisia.

The real conquest began in 825. Euphemius, the Byzantine admiral, finding himself threatened with imperial punishment for some offence, the nature of which is not quite clear, rebelled against the Emperor and seized the island. Later, when defeated by the Imperial forces, he fled to Tunisia with his ships and sought the aid of Ziyādatallah, the Aghlabid ruler of Tunisia, urging him to advance and conquer the island. Despite some hesitations the Tunisian ruler despatched a fleet of between seventy and one hundred vessels which effected a landing at Mazara in 827. After a rapid initial advance the invaders suffered some setbacks and were rescued from their difficulties only by the unexpected arrival of a band of adventurers from Spain. Thereafter the advance continued. In 831 the Muslims occupied Palermo, which became and remained the capital of the island throughout the period of Muslim rule and served as the base for further expansion. The war between the Byzantine and Muslim forces continued by land and sea on the island and on the Italian mainland until 895–6, when the Byzantines signed a peace by which they effectively renounced Sicily. The Muslims had captured Messina in ca. 843, Castrogiovanni in 859, and Syracuse in 878. Meanwhile they had landed on the mainland too, and established garrisons at Bari and Taranto for a time. Muslim raiders threatened Naples, Rome, and even northern Italy, and compelled one of the Popes to pay tribute for two years. Between 882 and 915 the Muslim military colony on the Garigliano terrorised Campagna and southern Latium. It may have been sent and maintained from Sicily.

Sicily under Muslim rule was at first a dependency of Tunisia, politically and administratively tied to that province. With the fall of the Aghlabids and their supersession by the Fāṭimids the sovereignty of the island passed to the new Caliphs. At first the governors of the island were directly appointed by the suzerain government or, in times of emergency, elected by the notables of Palermo. With the transfer of the Fāṭimids to Egypt in 972 the control of the central government weakened and the governorship became tacitly hereditary in the line of Ḥasan ibn 'Alī al-Kalbī. The hereditary governorship of the Kalbids, which lasted until 1040, marked the peak of Muslim power and influence on the island. The tenth-century traveller Ibn Ḥawqal found three hundred mosques in Palermo alone—an eloquent testimony to the extent of Muslim penetration. Later writers tell us of a rich efflorescence of Arabic culture and letters, of which unfortunately very little has survived.

The fall of the Kalbids was brought about by a civil war between Sicilian and African Muslims which ended the unity of the island. After a brief interval during which Palermo itself was ruled by a council of notables and the rest of the island by local princes, the Normans, who had meanwhile occupied southern Italy, invaded and captured the greater part of the island. In 1061 Roger I took Messina and by 1091 held all Sicily except for small outposts where the Muslims still held out. Under Norman rule, which lasted until 1194, an important part of the cultured town class migrated to North Africa and Egypt.

The Arabs in Sicily applied much the same principles of government as in the conquered lands of the East, and effected an important social change in the tenure and distribution of land. The survival of many Arab place names shows the intensity of Arab colonisation—the many Arabic words in the Sicilian dialect testify to their interest in agriculture. The Arabs brought to Sicily oranges, mulberries, sugar-cane, date-palms and cotton. They extended cultivation by careful irrigation, and to this day many fountains in Sicily, and especially in Palermo, still have easily recognisable Arab names. Monuments of Arab rule have almost all disappeared, and the books that the Arabs wrote in Sicily have survived only in fragments. The greatest of the Sicilian Arab poets, Ibn Ḥamdīs (*d.* 1132), has come down to us only in Spanish and Syrian copies of his writings. The causes of this disappearance are to be sought partly in the perishable materials used, partly in the emigration of the cultured classes that followed the Norman conquest, and above all in the destructive activities of the conquerors themselves.

But the Normans soon adapted themselves to the culture that they found in the island. Arab and Muslim elements in the court and culture of Norman Sicily are very numerous. Roger II (1130–1154), known as "The Pagan" because of his favouring of Muslims, used Arab troops and siege engineers in his campaigns in southern Italy and Arab architects for his buildings, who created the new and distinctive Saracenic-Norman style. His magnificent coronation mantle, woven in the royal *Ṭirāz* workshop of Palermo, bears an Arabic inscription in Kufic style and the Hijra date 528 (=1133–4). He retained even the Arab custom of maintaining court poets as eulogists. A later Muslim anthologist has preserved fragments of Arabic poems written in praise of this king and condemns the writers for demeaning themselves by eulogising infidels—"May God speedily plunge them into hottest hellfire." It was at Roger's court that Idrīsī, the greatest of the Arab geographers, wrote his monumental compendium of geography which he dedicated to the Norman king and which is known as *Kitāb Rujjār*—the Book of Roger. In 1185 the Spanish Muslim traveller Ibn Jubair visited the island. He remarks that the King (William II, 1166–1189) could read and write Arabic. "The King relies greatly on Muslims and entrusts to them his affairs, even the most important, so that the superintendent of his kitchen is a Muslim and . . . his Wazirs and chamberlains." The traveller remarks that even the Christians in Palermo looked and dressed like Muslims and spoke Arabic. The Norman kings continued to mint coins with Arabic inscriptions and Hijra dates, at first even with Muslim formulae. Many of the records were still kept in Arabic, including those of the courts.

At a later date, under the Swabian dynasty that followed the Normans, Latin gradually replaced Arabic in official usage and the last Arabic document in Sicily dates from 1242. But Arabic culture still survived and flourished under the rule of Frederick II (1215–1250), strengthened by his extensive dealings with the

Muslim Orient. Even under Manfred (*d.* 1266) signs of Arab influence are still visible, and at the camp of Lucera, the Sicilian Muslim colony established on the mainland by Frederick II, the five canonical prayers were still performed. But the old culture was dying out, and by the beginning of the fourteenth century Arabic was extinct in the island, while Islam was extirpated by emigration or apostasy. The place of Sicily in the transmission of Muslim culture to Europe is on the whole less than one would expect. Its main achievement dates from the reign of Frederick II, when a number of translators, Christian and Jewish, translated into Latin a series of Arabic works both original and based on Greek texts. Among them were Theodore, an astrologer of oriental origin, who translated works on hygiene and falconry, and the famous Michael Scot, a Scottish or Irish magician and astrologer who, after studying Arabic and Hebrew in Spain, entered the service of Frederick II in Sicily and remained there until his death. The last of the Sicilian translators was the Jewish doctor Faraj ibn Sālim, who translated a great medical work of Rāzī, the Rhases of the mediaeval West, into Latin for the Angevin King Charles I (*d.* 1285).

It was in Spain that the Arabs achieved their greatest and most enduring conquest in Europe. In the year 710 the Berber chief Ṭarīf, with the connivance of a rebellious Visigothic dignitary called Julian, led a raiding force across the Straits to Tarifa, which still bears his name. Encouraged by this success, Ṭāriq, a Berber freedman of Mūsā ibn Nuṣair, the Arab governor of north-west Africa, prepared a larger expedition, and in the spring of 711—with the help of Julian's ships—landed some 7000 men at Gibraltar (Jabal Ṭāriq). From there he advanced into the interior, defeating the Visigothic army and capturing Cordova and Toledo. The Muslim forces engaged hitherto had been almost exclusively Berber, but in 712 Mūsā himself arrived with a strong Arab force of some 10,000 men and seized the cities of Seville and Merida. Thereafter the Arab advance was rapid and by 718 they had occupied the greater part of the peninsula and crossed the Pyrenees into southern France, where their advance was only checked by the Franks under Charles Martel at the battle of Poitiers in 732.

Spain on the eve of the Arab conquests was in a weak and deplorable state. "Of all that she possessed once she retained only the name," says an early chronicler. On the one hand was a small landowning class with enormous latifundia, on the other a vast and miserable mass of serfs and slaves and a ruined and decayed middle class. The *Clarissimi*, or privileged class, were exempt from most taxes, luxurious and depraved; the rest were hungry and discontented. Around the countryside roved robber bands of runaway serfs and slaves. In 616 an intense persecution of the numerous Jews of the peninsula began, adding one more element to the many who had nothing to lose and all to gain from any change. The Visigoth army consisted largely of conscript serfs. Its unreliability is easily understandable. The initial victories of the Arabs brought about the almost immediate collapse of the wormeaten structure of the Visigoth state. The serfs went on strike; the Jews revolted and joined the invaders, handing over the city of Toledo to them.

The new regime was liberal and tolerant, and even the Spanish chroniclers describe it as preferable to the Frankish rule in the north. The greatest benefit that it brought to the country was the elimination of the old ruling class of nobility and clergy and the distribution of their lands, creating a new class of smallholders who were largely responsible for the agricultural prosperity of Muslim Spain. The serfs were far better off, while the *bourgeoisie* found a refuge from its troubles in large-scale conversion to Islam and in identifying itself with the Arabs.

After the conquests the soldiers of the invading armies remained in Spain, where they settled and intermarried. New waves of immigration from North Africa and the East followed during the eighth century, bringing many Arabs and even more Africans into the peninsula. In 741 the Berbers were strong enough to stage a general revolt in Spain against the Arabs. The Caliph sent an Arab and largely Syrian army which arrived in 742 after a long and adventurous journey, under the command of Balj ibn Bishr. It soon defeated the Berbers and in reward received the Mediterranean coastlands of Spain in fief. These new colonists from Syria were settled on the same plan as in Syria itself, and a Spanish district was allocated to the men of each of the Syrian *Junds* (military districts)—Damascus in Elvira, the Jordan at Malaga, Palestine in Sidonia, Ḥims in Seville, Qinnasrin in Jaen. The army of Egypt held Beja and Murcia. These Arab fief-holders were liable for military service on the summons of the government in Cordova, the Arab capital. Otherwise they were supposed to live on their lands. But the Arabs had not yet taken to agriculture, and the fief-holders for the most part preferred to settle in the chief towns of the districts in which their lands were situated and to live on the revenues they drew from Spanish serfs or share-croppers who cultivated their estates. They formed a new town population, an Arab warrior caste living on their revenues and known as *Shāmīs*, or Syrians, to distinguish them from the older settlers who had come with the first invasion.

The strengthening of the Syrian element in Spain by these events created a favourable atmosphere for 'Abd ar-Raḥmān, an Umayyad prince fleeing from the ruin of his house in the east. After some preparatory work among the army of Balj, many of whom were former Umayyad clients, he landed at Almuñecar in 755. He soon defeated the governor who had recognised the 'Abbāsids, and, seizing Cordova in 756, established the independent Umayyad dynasty in Spain which was to last until 1031.

The first century of Umayyad rule in Spain was a period of troubles, during which the Amīrs of Cordova were busy pacifying the country and dealing with latent and open insurrection from the various elements of the population. The Arabs were mainly townsmen, the great vassals of the Jund military aristocracy. They were strongest in the south-east and for a while offered a grave threat to the authority of the government. The cessation of Arab immigration during the ninth century and the progressive fusion between the Arabs and the Arabised Spanish converts to Islam gradually weakened the influence of the great Arab families, who in later Umayyad times ceased to play any significant role in public affairs. Far more numerous and far more dangerous were the Berbers, whose numbers increased by constant immigration until as late as the eleventh century. In the towns they formed a minority, rapidly assimilated. The majority of them, mountaineers from Morocco, preferred to settle in the mountain districts, attracted by the congenial way of life based on livestock and agriculture and the military advantages of the familiar type of terrain. Finally, there were the Spaniards themselves, Christian, Jewish, and converts. The non-Muslim protected communities were more numerous and better organised in Spain than anywhere else in Islam. The policy of the government towards them was generally liberal and tolerant, such repression as occurred being due largely to political considerations. But conversion to Islam, induced by attraction rather than by coercion, was rapid and extensive. Soon the Arabic-speaking Spanish Muslims, free, freedmen and slaves, formed a major part of the population. Even those who remained faithful to their old religions adopted Arabic to a remarkable extent. As early as the middle of the ninth century Alvaro, a Christian of Cordova, remarks with regret:

> "Many of my co-religionists read the poetry and tales of the Arabs, study the writings of Muhammadan theologians and philosophers, not in order to refute them, but to learn how to express themselves in Arabic with greater correctness and elegance. Where can one find today a layman who reads the Latin commentaries on the Holy Scriptures? Who among them studies the Gospels, the Prophets, the Apostles? All the young Christians noted for their gifts know only the language and literature of the Arabs, read and study with zeal Arabic books, building up great libraries of them at enormous cost and loudly proclaiming everywhere that this literature is worthy of admiration. Among thousands of us there is hardly one who can write a passable Latin letter to a friend, but innumerable are those who can express themselves in Arabic and compose poetry in that language with greater art than the Arabs themselves."

At about the same time the Archbishop of Seville deemed it necessary to translate and annotate the Bible in Arabic, not for missionary purposes but for his own community. Many Christians worked in the service of the state and even bishops were sent by the Umayyad Amīrs on important diplomatic missions. The term Mozarab—from the Arabic ***Musta'rib*** (arabising)—was used to describe the Arabic-speaking Christians and Jews. The converts are known in Spanish history as renegades, in Arabic as ***Muwallad***, roughly, adopted.

The reign of 'Abd ar-Raḥmān II (822–852) was a relatively long period of peace. 'Abd ar-Raḥmān reorganised the Cordovan realm on 'Abbāsid models, introducing a centralised and bureaucratic administration and the 'Abbāsid organisation of the court. He was noted as a patron of letters who brought many books and scholars from the East, greatly strengthening the cultural connections between Spanish Islam and the centres of Islamic civilisation in the Orient. One of the most noteworthy figures among them was Ziryāb, a Persian musician driven from the court of Hārūn ar-Rashīd by the jealousy of his teacher. He found a refuge at the Court of Cordova. Ziryāb became the unquestioned arbiter of taste and fashion in the Spanish capital, introducing many new and unknown refinements of Eastern civilisation, ranging from the oriental musical modes to wearing fine robes and eating asparagus.

Under the successors of 'Abd ar-Raḥmān the menace of internal dissension dwindled. Arabs, Berbers and Spanish Muslims gradually fused into a homogeneous Muslim population, proud of its independence in culture and politics, increasingly Iberian in outlook. This movement towards political and cultural unification benefited greatly from the turn of events at the beginning of the tenth century. The rise of the Fāṭimids in North Africa and the establishment of a schismatic anti-Caliphate at the head of a widespread and seditious revolutionary movement led the Amīr 'Abd ar-Raḥmān III (912–961) to assume for himself the title and dignity of Caliph, thereby proclaiming himself supreme religious head of the Muslims of Spain and severing the last bonds of subjection to the East. The Caliphate of 'Abd ar-Raḥmān III began the

Umayyad apogee. His reign was a period of political stability and internal peace in which both Arab feudal chiefs and Berber mountaineers were firmly subjected to the central government. Eastern influences dwindled and a distinctive Hispano-Arab civilisation began to emerge in which the classical Arab tradition was subjected to the subtle influences of the local environment. At the same time trade relations with the East were maintained and the opening of diplomatic relations with Byzantium indicates the power and prestige of the Umayyad state. Al-Ḥakam II (961–976), a famous Maecenas who built up a library of many thousand volumes, and especially his wazīr Al-Manṣūr—or Almanzor—the real ruler of the country, continued the work of 'Abd ar-Raḥmān in centralising the government and unifying the population.

The death of Al-Manṣūr during the reign of Hishām (976–1008) was followed by a break-up. The relaxation of central control released the pent-up rivalries between the two parties, the "Andalusian", that is to say the whole of the Muslim population of Spain, and the Berbers of recent immigration from Africa. In the interlude of civil war and dissension that followed, a third party, known as the Slavs, played a fateful role. This term was applied at first to slaves of east European origin, eventually to all slaves of European origin in the Royal service. Many of them were Italian or came from the still unconquered strongholds of independent Christianity in the north. They were imported at an early age and were mainly Muslim and Arabic-speaking. By the middle of the ninth century they were of growing importance in both the army and the palace and under 'Abd ar-Raḥmān III are quoted as numbering 13,750. Many were liberated and acquired wealth and status. Umayyad princes had used them to counteract the influence of the Arab feudal chiefs, appointing many of them to high posts in the government and to army commands. Their insubordination and their conflicts with the Berbers helped greatly to bring about the overthrow of the Umayyad Caliphate.

The first half of the eleventh century was a period of political fragmentation, during which Muslim Spain was divided among a series of petty kings and princes of Berber, Slav or Andalusian origin, known as the "party kings". This political weakness led to a double invasion of Muslim Spain by Christians from the north with Frankish assistance, and by Berbers from the south. In 1085 the advancing tide of Christian reconquest engulfed the city of Toledo, the loss of which was a crushing blow to Spanish Islam. Yet despite the political weakness and disunity of the country the interlude of the "party kings" was a period of great cultural efflorescence. The many petty courts were centres of scholarship, philosophy, science and literature, while the fall of the Caliphate permitted the resumption of active relations, both economic and cultural, with the East.

The reign of the "party kings" was ended by a new Berber invasion from Africa. Yūsuf ibn Tashfīn, the founder of the Almoravid dynasty, entered Spain at the invitation of the Andalusians themselves in order to meet the Christian menace. Defeating the Christians in 1086, he proceeded to annex the party monarchies to his Moorish Empire. The Almoravids in turn gave way to the new African dynasty of the Almohades, a fanatical Berber sect. Meanwhile the Christian reconquest continued. In 1195 the Muslims won their last major victory at Alarcos. In 1212 the Muslim defeat of Las Navas de Tolosa initiated a series of Christian advances culminating in the capture of Cordova in 1236 and of Seville in 1248. The Almoravid Kingdom broke up into a new series of party monarchies of short duration. By the end of the thirteenth century the Christians had reconquered the whole of the peninsula with the exception only of the city and province of Granada, where for nearly two centuries more a Muslim dynasty ruled. It was there, in the sunset glow of Spanish Islam, that rose the magnificent fantasy of the Alhambra, the last and supreme expression of its creative genius. On the 2nd January, 1492, the combined armies of Castile and Aragon captured the city of Granada, and shortly after a Royal edict decreed the expulsion of all non-Catholics from the peninsula. The Arabic language lingered on for a while among forced converts to Christianity, but even these were deported to Africa at the beginning of the seventeenth century.

Spanish Islam at its peak presented a proud spectacle. The Arabs enriched the life of the peninsula in many ways: in agriculture they introduced scientific irrigation and a number of new crops including citrus fruits, cotton, sugar-cane and rice. The changes which they wrought in the system of land tenure were largely responsible for the prosperous state of Spanish agriculture under Arab rule. They developed many industries—textiles, pottery, paper, silk, and sugar-refining, and opened important mines of gold, silver and other metals. Wool and silk were manufactured in Cordova, Malaga and Almeria, pottery in Malaga and Valencia, arms in Cordova and Toledo, leather in Cordova, carpets in Beza and Calcena, paper—an Arab introduction from the Further East—in Jativa and Valencia. As elsewhere in Islam, textiles were the chief industry, and we hear of 13,000 weavers in Cordova alone. Muslim Spain carried on an extensive foreign trade with the East, and merchant fleets based on the Andalusian ports carried Spanish goods all over the Mediterranean. The chief markets were in North Africa and above all Egypt, and in Constantinople, where Byzantine merchants purchased their products and resold them to India and Central Asia. The many Arabic words surviving in agriculture and in the crafts show the strength of Arab influence. Even in political life the many Arabic terms still used in Spanish in local administration and in the military vocabulary testify to the persistence of the Arab tradition. The fourteenth-century Christian king who restored the Alcazar in Seville commemorated his work in an inscription in Arabic, "Glory to our Lord, the Sultan Don Pedro". The coins of the reconquest remained Arab in pattern for a long time.

Spanish Islam made important contributions to every branch of the main classical Arab tradition, to which, despite its remoteness and its local characteristics, it ultimately belonged. Even the Greek heritage reached the Spanish Arabs from the East through books imported from the Eastern centres of translation, notably during the reign of 'Abd ar-Raḥmān II, rather than from local sources. Local influence made itself felt primarily in lyrical poetry, where the Spanish Arabs created new forms unknown to the Muslim East, which had a considerable influence on early Spanish Christian poetry and possibly also on the other literatures of western Europe. Perhaps the most distinctive creation of Spanish Islam was its art and architecture, based initially on the Arab and Byzantine models of the Near East and developed under local influences into something new, individual and original. The famous mosque of Cordova, begun under 'Abd ar-Raḥmān I, marks the starting point of the new Hispano-Moorish style, which was later to produce masterpieces like the Giralda Tower and Alcazar in Seville and the Alhambra of Granada.

The Spanish historians, as may be expected, are not uniformly enthusiastic about the permanent effects of the Arab occupation on Spanish life and institutions. In a thoughtful essay the modern Spanish scholar Sanchez Albornoz enumerates what are in his view the lasting harmful results of the long vigil of Christian Spain as sentinel of the West against the advance of Islam and of the sustained effort of the reconquest. The first of these is the political fragmentation of the country. The conquest and reconquest nullified the political unification of the peninsula, far advanced under Roman rule, and through the piecemeal reconquest revived the old Spanish spirit of particularism and caused Spain to lag far behind the rest of Europe in political development and centralisation. Parallel with this was the economic backwardness bequeathed to Christian Spain by the absorption of all available energy in the great task of the reconquest, leaving little or none for the development of trade and industry which were in any case dislocated by the transfer of Spain from the African and Mediterranean orbit, to which it belonged during the period of Arab rule, to that of western Europe, where it was a newcomer, behind the rest on the path of development and unhappily placed on the periphery. Finally, he remarks, "the fatal influence of Saracen domination in Spain retarded not only economic life and political organisation. Even in the most intimate fibres of the Spanish soul it produced reactions pregnant with sad corollaries". The sustained effort of the reconquest gave rise to a warlike and adventurous mentality and an attenuation of political sense which led the Spaniards to squander their energies in fruitless campaigns of imperial expansion, while the religious character of the war produced the unhealthy overgrowth of the clergy and clerical influence which has been the bane of Spanish political life. A point sometimes made by Spanish scholars is that while the civilisation of the Caliphate was undoubtedly rich and varied—richer, indeed, than any other in western Europe at the time—it did not compensate for these injuries, since most of it was banished from the country along with the Arabs themselves and percolated only to a limited extent to the cultural life of Christian Spain, which was based far more on the poor and backward independent states of the unconquered north than on the splendid culture of the Muslim south.

It is true that the permanent influence of the Arabs on Spain was far smaller than, for example, on Persia. In Persian, almost the whole terminology of cultural and spiritual life is still Arabic. In Spanish, it is Latin. But even the many surviving words relating to material life show the important debt of Spain to the Arabs in economic, social and, to some extent also, in political matters. In culture, too, the Arab heritage must be regarded as of great importance to Spain, and indeed to all western Europe. Christians from many countries came to Spain to study together with the native Spaniards under Arabic-speaking Muslim and Jewish teachers, and translated many books from Arabic into Latin. A great part of the legacy of ancient Greece first became known to the West in the Arabic translations found in Spain. The first great centre for the transmission of culture from Islam to Christianity in the West was the city of Toledo, reconquered in 1085. Many learned Muslims remained in the city and were soon reinforced by numbers of Jewish refugees from the Muslim south, now under the rule of the intolerant Almohades, who introduced violent religious persecution into Muslim Spain and drove many Jews to seek a temporary refuge in the more liberal atmosphere of Toledo. During the twelfth and thirteenth centuries, and especially during the reign of Alfonso the Wise of Castile and Leon (1252–1284), the Toledo schools of translators produced a great corpus of works including the *Organon* of Aristotle and many of the writings of Euclid, Ptolemy, Galen, and Hippocrates, enriched by their Arabic commentators and successors. The translators usually worked with bilingual natives, many of them Jewish, and included both Spanish and foreign scholars. Among them were Domingo Gundisalvi, converted Jews like John of Seville and Petrus Alphonsi, and, from other countries, Gerard of Cremona from Italy, Herman the Dalmatian from Germany, Adelard of Bath, Daniel of Morlay and Michael Scot from Britain.

The Arabs left their mark on Spain—in the skills of the Spanish peasant and craftsman and the words with which he describes them, in the art, architecture, music and literature of the peninsula, and in the science and philosophy of the mediaeval West which they had enriched by the transmission of the legacy of antiquity faithfully guarded and increased. Among the Arabs themselves the memory of Muslim Spain survived among the exiles in North Africa, many of whom still bear Andalusian names and keep the keys of their houses in Cordova and Seville hanging on their walls in Marrakesh and in Casablanca. In more recent times visitors to Spain from the East, like the Egyptian poet Aḥmad Shawqī and the Syrian scholar Muḥammad Kurd 'Alī, have reminded the Arabs of the Orient of the great achievements of their Spanish brothers and restored the memory of Spanish Islam to its rightful place in the national consciousness of the Arabs.

VIII

ISLAMIC CIVILISATION

"*The sciences were transmitted into the Arabic language from different parts of the world; by it they were embellished and penetrated the hearts of men, while the beauties of that language flowed in their veins and arteries.*"

(Al-Bīrūnī, *Kitāb as-Saidana*)

DURING the period of greatness of the Arab and Islamic Empires in the Near and Middle East a flourishing civilisation grew up that is usually known as Arabic. It was not brought ready-made by the Arab invaders from the desert, but was created after the conquests by the collaboration of many peoples, Arabs, Persians, Egyptians and others. Nor was it even purely Muslim, for many Christians, Jews and Zoroastrians were among its creators. But its chief medium of expression was Arabic, and it was dominated by Islam and its outlook on life. It was these two things, their language and their faith, which were the great contributions of the Arab invaders to the new and original civilisation which developed under their aegis.

Arabic is one of the Semitic languages, in many ways the richest of them. The pre-Islamic Arabs had been a primitive people with a hard and primitive way of life, little education or formal culture, hardly any written tradition. But they had developed a poetic language and tradition of remarkable richness, a poetry of elaborate and intricate metre, rhyme and diction, classical exactitude of form, which was the pattern for most later Arabic poetry. With its wealth of passion and image and its limitation of themes it is the true expression of the life of the Bedouins, singing of wine, love, war, hunting, the terrible landscapes of mountain and desert, the martial valour of the tribesmen themselves, the turpitude of their enemies. As one would expect, it is not a literature of abstraction or pure thought.

The conquests made Arabic an imperial language, soon also the language of a great and diverse culture. Arabic expanded to meet these two needs, partly by borrowing new words and expressions, but mainly by development from within, forming new words from old roots, giving new meanings to old words. As an example of the process we may choose the Arabic word for "absolute", a notion quite unnecessary to the pre-Islamic Arabs. It is *mujarrad*, the passive participle of *jarrada*, to strip bare or denude, a term normally used of locusts and connected with the words *jarāda*, locust, and *jarīda*, leaf. The language created in this way possessed a vivid, concrete and pictorial vocabulary, with each term having deep roots in a purely Arab past and tradition. It allowed of the direct and uncushioned impact of ideas on the mind through concrete and familiar words and of unrestricted penetration to and from the deeper layers of consciousness.

The Arabic language, thus enriched, remained the sole instrument of culture for long after the fall of the purely Arab kingdom. With the language of the Arabs came their poetry as its classical model and the world of ideas embedded therein—concrete, not abstract, though often subtle and allusive; rhetorical and declamatory, not intimate and personal; recitative and spasmodic, not epic and sustained; a literature where the impact of words and form counted for more than the transmission of ideas.

It was the Arabisation of the conquered provinces rather than their military conquest that is the true wonder of the Arab expansion. By the eleventh century Arabic had become not only the chief idiom of everyday use from Persia to the Pyrenees, but also the chief instrument of culture, superseding old culture languages like Coptic, Aramaic, Greek and Latin. As the Arabic language spread, the distinction between Arab conqueror and Arabised conquered faded into relative insignificance, and while all who spoke Arabic and professed Islam were felt to belong to a single community the term Arab was restricted once again to the nomads who had originally borne it or was used as a title of aristocratic descent with no great economic or social significance.

Even beyond the vast areas that were permanently Arabised, Arabic exercised a tremendous influence on other Muslim languages. Muslim Persian and Turkish, and later also Urdu, Malay and Swahili, are new languages written in the Arabic script and including an enormous Arabic vocabulary, as great as the Greek and Latin elements in English, and covering the whole world of concepts and ideas.

The survival and expansion of Arabic involved more than the language itself—more, for example, than the continued use of Latin in the mediaeval West. With the language came Arab taste and tradition in the choice and treatment of themes. It is illuminating to contrast the poetry written in Arabic by Persians until the eleventh century with poetry written in Persian at a later date when Muslim Persia developed an independent Islamic culture of its own. Persian Arabic poetry differs in many important respects from the early poetry of the Arabs themselves, yet basically conforms to Arab taste and is still treasured by the Arabs as part of their heritage. It is lacking in the epic and in the subjective lyricism of later Persian poetry.

Islam—the offspring of Arabia and the Arabian Prophet—was not only a system of belief and cult. It was also a system of state, society, law, thought and art—a civilisation with religion as its unifying, eventually dominating, factor. From the Hijra onwards Islam meant submission not only to the new faith, but to the community—in practice, to the suzerainty of Medina and the Prophet, later of the Empire and Caliph. Islam was at first Arab citizenship, later the first-class citizenship of the Empire. Its code was the *Sharī'a*, the holy law developed by jurists from the Qur'ān and the traditions of the Prophet. The *Sharī'a* was not only a normative code of law but also, in its social and political aspects, a pattern of conduct, an ideal towards which men and society must strive. Islam admitted no legislative power since law could emanate only from God through revelation, but customary law and civil legislation, the will of the ruler, survived unofficially with occasional limited recognition from the jurists. The divinely granted *Sharī'a* regulated every aspect of life, not only belief and cult, but also public law, constitutional and international, and private law, criminal and civil. Its ideal character is clearest in its constitutional aspect. According to the *Sharī'a*, the head of the community is the Caliph, an elected vicegerent of God with supreme power in all military, civil and religious matters and with the duty of maintaining intact the spiritual and material legacy of the Prophet. The Caliph had no spiritual powers himself. He could not change doctrine, nor create new doctrine; he was supported by no priesthood, but only by the semi-clerical class of the '*Ulamā*', the doctors of the divine law whose powers were limited to interpretation. In practice, the Caliph became the puppet of military commanders and political adventurers who, from the ninth century onwards, were the real rulers of Islam. By the eleventh century the Sultan emerged as supreme secular ruler alongside the Caliph, with powers recognised *post facto* and reluctantly by the jurists. In the administration of law we see the same contrast. Alongside the Qāḍī, administering the Holy Law, there were secular courts, the ostensible purpose of which was to deal with matters not falling within the Qāḍī's jurisdiction and to remedy injustices by the use of discretionary powers.

Both these gifts of the Arab, his language and his faith, were of course subject from the earliest times to external influences. There are foreign words even in pre-Islamic poetry and in the Qur'ān, many more in the period of the conquests. Administrative terms from Persian and Greek, theological and religious terms from Hebrew and Syriac, scientific and philosophic terms from Greek show the immense influence of the older civilisations of the area on the new one that was being born. Islamic society of the classical period was a complex development incorporating within itself many elements of diverse origin: Christian, Jewish and Zoroastrian ideas of prophecy, legal religion, eschatology and mysticism, Sasanid and Byzantine administrative and imperial practices. Perhaps the most important was the impact of Hellenism, especially in science, philosophy, art and architecture, and even to some slight extent in literature. So great is the Hellenistic influence that Islam has been described as the third heir, alongside Greek and Latin Christendom, of the Hellenistic legacy. But the Hellenism of Islam was the later Near Eastern Hellenism, semi-orientalised by Aramaic and Christian influences, the uninterrupted continuation of late antiquity rather than a rediscovery, as in the West, of classical Athens.

Despite this diversity of its origins Islamic civilisation was no mere mechanical juxtaposition of previous cultures, but rather a new creation, in which all these elements were fused into a new and original civilisation by the transposition into Arabic and Islamic forms, recognisable and characteristic in every phase of its achievement.

The highest achievement of the Arabs in their own reckoning and the first in order of time was poetry, with the allied art of rhetoric. Pre-Islamic poetry had had a public and social function, with the poet often appearing as eulogist or satirist, with an important political role. Under the Umayyads the orally transmitted poetry of pre-Islamic Arabia was codified and served as the model for further development. Under the 'Abbāsids Arabic poetry was enriched by the accession of many non-Arabs, especially Persians, the first of whom to achieve greatness was the blind and gifted Bashshār ibn Burd (*d.* 784). These for a while gained a victory for new themes and forms over the pre-Islamic models in a bitterly fought struggle of ancients and moderns. But even these innovators were limited by the need to accommodate themselves to the Arab tastes of the rulers and the governing *élite* and eventually gave way before a triumph of neo-classicism, the most distinguished exponent of which was Mutanabbī (905–965), regarded by the Arabs as the greatest of their poets.

The Qur'ān itself is the first document of Arab prose literature, which in the early centuries of Islamic rule developed both prose and rhymed prose and was richest in *belles lettres* and in essay. The greatest master of the essay and indeed of Arabic prose was 'Amr ibn Baḥr, known as al-Jāḥiẓ, "the goggle-eyed" (*d.* 869). A native of Baṣra and the grandson of a negro slave, his versatility, originality and charm give him a unique place in Arabic letters. Science and learning were religious in origin. Grammar and lexicography arose from the need to interpret and explain the Qur'ān. In Medina the pietists of the old school concentrated on the religious sciences proper—the interpretation of the Qur'ān, the formulation of dogma, and the codification of the Tradition. The last gave rise to the Islamic schools of jurisprudence and history, developed from the legal and biographical material of the Tradition. The former grew into the elaborate juristic Codex of the Sharī'a. History among the Arabs began with the biography of the Prophet, enriched by the codification of the pre-Islamic oral historical tradition of the Arabs and later more especially by the example of the Persian court chroniclers of the Sasanids, introduced to the Arabs by Persian converts. The Arabs have a strong historical sense and were soon producing voluminous histories of many kinds: universal histories, local histories, histories of families, tribes and institutions. The earliest Arab historical works are little more than source books written in the manner of the compendia of Tradition, consisting of eye-witness accounts introduced by a chain of transmitting authorities. From these, narrative and occasionally interpretative, history developed, culminating in the work of Ibn Khaldūn (1332–1406), the greatest historian of the Arabs and perhaps the greatest historical thinker of the Middle Ages.

Religious literature was subject to strong Christian and Jewish influence, especially in the early period, and much apocalyptic and talmudic material was incorporated into the Tradition. Theological literature proper began under the influences of Syriac Christianity, later also of Greek thought. Greek influence was fundamental in philosophy and all the sciences: mathematics, astronomy, geography, chemistry, physics, natural history and medicine. The immense effort of translation of Greek books either directly from the original or from Syriac versions produced a new growth of learning in the ninth and tenth centuries. Greek schools had survived in Alexandria, Antioch and elsewhere, and in the Persian college of Jundaishapur founded by Nestorian refugees from Byzantium in Sasanid Persia. The movement of translation began under the Umayyads, when some Greek and Coptic works on chemistry were translated. Under 'Umar II, Māsarjawaih, a Jew of

Baṣra, translated Syriac medical books into Arabic, laying the foundations of Arab medical science. The translators were usually Christians and Jews, mainly Syrian. Under the Umayyads, translation was sporadic and individual; under the 'Abbāsids it was organised and officially encouraged. The greatest period was the ninth century and especially the reign of Ma'mūn (813–833), who established a school for translators in Baghdad with a library and a regular staff. One of the most notable translators was Ḥunain ibn Iṣḥāq (*ca.* 809–877), a Christian doctor of Jundaishapur, who translated the Corpus of Galen, the *Aphorisms* of Hippocrates, and many other works. Other translators dealt with astronomy, physics, mathematics and other subjects, translating them from Greek into Syriac and more frequently into Arabic. The Caliphs sent scholars to different places and even to Byzantium in search of manuscripts.

Some of these early translators also produced works of their own, usually summaries and interpretations of Greek originals. But soon a generation of original Muslim writers arose, mainly Persian, including such figures as the physician Rāzī (Rhases) (865–925), the physician and philosopher Ibn Sīnā (Avicenna) (980–1037), and, greatest of all, Al-Bīrūnī, (973–1048), physician, astronomer, mathematician, physicist, chemist, geographer and historian, a profound and original scholar, who was one of the greatest intellectual figures in mediaeval Islam. In medicine, the Arabs did not touch the basic theory of the Greeks, but enriched it by practical observation and clinical experience. In mathematics, physics and chemistry their contribution was far greater and more original. The use of the Zero, and the so-called Arabic numerals, though not an original Arab invention, was first incorporated into the main body of mathematical theory by them and transmitted from India to Europe. Algebra and geometry, and especially trigonometry, were largely Arabic developments.

In philosophy, the introduction of Greek ideas was of transcending importance. They first came into their own under Ma'mūn, when translations of Aristotle affected the whole philosophy and theological outlook of Islam and influenced the works of a long series of original Muslim thinkers, among whom we may name Kindī (*d. ca.* 850)—incidentally, the only pure Arab among them—Fārābī (*d.* 950), Ibn Sīnā (*d.* 1037), and Ibn Rushd (Averroes) (*d.* 1198).

It is usually asserted that whereas the East alone had preserved the scientific and philosophic heritage of ancient Greece it ignored the literary and aesthetic heritage, which was known only in the West. This is not wholly true. The Arabs continued the tradition of Greco-Roman art and architecture, which again they transmuted into something rich and strange. The tendency of Byzantine art towards the abstract and the formal was increased in Islam, where the prejudice against the pictorial representation of the human form led ultimately to an art of stylised and geometrical design.

The Islamic arts also owe a great deal to Persian and Chinese influences and contributions. In the decorative and industrial arts we can see most clearly both the eclecticism and the originality of Islamic civilisation. On the walls of the Umayyad castles of Syria, in the excavated utensils and other objects of Iraq and Egypt, we see how the Arabs first borrowed the works of art—and even the artists—of other civilisations, then imitated them separately, finally fused them into something new, original and self-reproducing. The pottery finds of ninth-century Iraq, for example, show side by side the continued output of Byzantine and Sasanid craftsmanship, imported articles from China, local imitations of these, and new developments by experiment with inherited and imported models. One of the characteristic achievements of Islamic art is its famous and beautiful lustred pottery, that spread under Muslim rule from Persia to Spain. In the same way the craftsmen of the Islamic Empire developed the arts of metal, wood, stone, ivory, glass, and above all textiles and carpets, from borrowing, through imitation and experiment, to the creation of new, individual and characteristic styles, recognisably and distinctively Islamic.

From the older civilisations came too the very idea of the book as a physical entity, a bound collection of pages with title, subject, beginning and end, later with illustrations and ornamented bindings. A work of literature in Arabic was at first published only by oral transmission and recitation, and for a long time the spoken word was the only recognised form of publication. With the great increase in the range and size of literary creations written texts became necessary, and soon authors made drafts, lectured, dictated, employed amanuenses, and, eventually, wrote books. The process was helped by the introduction of paper from China in the eighth century, via Central Asia. This made possible cheaper and more extensive book production, and in its effect on cultural life is comparable, albeit on a much smaller scale, with the later extension of printing in the West.

The acceptance of the Greek heritage by Islam gave rise to a struggle between the scientific rationalist tendency of the new learning on the one hand, and the atomistic and intuitive quality of Islamic thought on the other. During the period of struggle Muslims of both schools created a rich and varied culture, much of which is of permanent importance in the history of mankind. The struggle ended in the victory of the more purely Islamic point of view. Islam, a religiously conditioned society, rejected values that challenged its fundamental postulates, while accepting their results, and even developing them by experiment and observation. Ismāʿīlism—the *révolution manquée* of Islam—might have ushered in a full acceptance of Hellenistic values, heralding a humanist renaissance of the Western type, overcoming the resistance of the Qur'ān by the device of esoteric interpretation, of the *Sharīʿa* by the unbounded discretion of the infallible Imām. But the forces supporting the Ismāʿīlī revolution were not strong enough, and it failed in the very moment of its greatest success.

It is a fruitless if pleasant pastime to analyse the characters of nations—one that usually throws more light on the analyst than on the subject analysed. The nation is far too complex, too diverse an organism, to admit of the detailed statistical examination which alone could substantiate any serious scientific statement. Still greater is the difficulty in dealing with a civilisation remote from us in time and space, known chiefly from its literary remains. Mediaeval Arabic literature comes almost entirely from the small privileged ruling minority whose privileges included the art of writing and the exercise of patronage. The rest, the common people, are for ever silent, except for such few echoes of their voices as can still be dimly heard. But with this reservation in mind it is still possible to isolate certain characteristics that are typical, if not of the Arabs, at least of the dominant civilisation of mediaeval Islam as exposed in Arab art and letters.

The first feature that strikes us is the unique assimilative power of Arab culture, often misrepresented as merely imitative. The Arab conquests united, for the first time in history, the vast territories stretching from the borders of India and China to the approaches of Greece, Italy and France. For a while by their military and political power, for much longer by their language and faith, the Arabs united in a single society two formerly conflicting cultures—the millennial and diversified Mediterranean tradition of Greece, Rome, Israel and the ancient Near East, and the rich civilisation of Persia, with its own patterns of life and thought and its fruitful contacts with the great cultures of the remoter East. Of the cohabitation of many peoples, faiths and cultures within the confines of the Islamic society a new civilisation was born, diverse in its origins and its creators, yet bearing on all its manifestations the characteristic imprint of Arabic Islam.

From this diversity of Islamic society arises a second feature, particularly striking to the European observer—its comparative tolerance. Unlike his Western contemporaries, the mediaeval Muslim rarely felt the need to impose his faith by force on all who were subject to his rule. Like them, he knew well enough that in due time those who believed differently would burn in Hell. Unlike them, he saw no point in anticipating the divine judgment in this world. At most times he was content to be of the dominant faith in a society of many faiths. He imposed on the others certain social and legal disabilities in token of his primacy, and gave them an effective reminder if ever they seemed disposed to forget. Otherwise he left them their religious, economic and intellectual freedom, and the opportunity to make a notable contribution to his own civilisation.

Like almost all other civilisations, mediaeval Islam was transcendently convinced of its own superiority and, in essentials, self-sufficiency. The Islamic historical view of prophecy, according to which the mission of Muḥammad was the last link in a chain of revelation of which Judaism and Christianity are the earlier links, enabled the Muslim to regard the Jew and the Christian as the possessors of early and imperfect versions of something which he alone possessed in its perfection. Unlike Christianity, which spread for centuries as the religion of the humble and dispossessed before becoming the state faith of the Roman Empire, Islam became during the lifetime of its founder the guiding code of an expanding and victorious community. The immense conquests of Islam in the first formative generations imprinted on the minds of the Believers the conviction of divine favour as expressed by the power and success in this world of the only community that lived by the God-given law. Muslims might learn much from wise infidels of other faiths, but the final touchstone of the validity of the lesson was the *Sharī'a*, hallowed by direct revelation and confirmed by the success of its followers.

The word "atomistic" is often used to describe a habit of mind and outlook, recognisable in many aspects of the civilisation of the Arab and dominant in the later stages of his history. By this is meant the tendency to view life and the universe as a series of static, concrete and disjunct entities, loosely linked in a sort of mechanical or even casual association by circumstances or the mind of an individual, but having no organic interrelation of their own. Though by no means universal, this tendency affects the life of the Arab in many different ways. He conceives his society not as an organic whole, compounded of interrelated and interacting parts, but as an association of separate groups—religions, nations, classes—held together only by the ground beneath and the government above. His town is an agglomeration of quarters, guilds, clans, houses, only rarely with any corporate civic identity of its own. In contrast to the scientists and philosophers on the one hand and the mystics on the other, the ordinary orthodox theologian, scholar or *littérateur* shows the same quality in his attitude to knowledge.

The various disciplines are not different ways of reaching out towards the same heart, pooling their findings in an integrated whole, but separate and self-contained compartments, each holding a finite number of pieces of knowledge, the progressive accumulation of which constitutes learning. Arabic literature, devoid of epic or drama, achieves its effects by a series of separate observations or characterisations, minute and vivid, but fragmentary, linked by the subjective associations of author and reader, rarely by an overriding plan. The Arabic poem is a set of separate and detachable lines, strung pearls that are perfect in themselves, usually interchangeable. Arabic music is modal and rhythmic, developed by fantasy and variation, never by harmony. Arabic art—mainly applied and decorative—is distinguished by its minuteness and perfection of detail rather than by composition or perspective. The historians and biographers, like the fiction writers, present their narrative as a series of loosely connected incidents. Even the individual is drawn as a sum of attributes, often listed, as a recent writer remarks, like the description on a passport.

This last brings us to another point, the impersonality—even collectivism—that is a recurring feature of Arabic prose literature. The fiery individualism of the early Arabs survived in full vigour among only the Bedouin, giving way in the centres of civilisation to a passive and even anonymous attitude. A book is often presented not as an individual and personal creation of the author, but as a link in the chain of transmission, the author concealing his own personality behind the prestige of authority and the ranks of previous transmitters. Even poetry, essentially an individual expression, is public and social rather than personal and intimate. This collectivist, rather than humanist, approach appears in every facet of Islamic thought and institutions, perhaps most clearly in the Muslim ideal of the Perfect Man and the Perfect State as externally applied patterns to which all must in theory attempt to conform by imitation rather than by developing their own individual potentialities from within.

The atomistic outlook on life received its complete expression in certain systems of dogmatic theology, the general acceptance of which in one form or another marks the final victory of the reaction against the freer spirit of speculation and enquiry that had produced such magnificent achievements. This theology is determinist, occasionalist and authoritarian, demanding the unquestioning acceptance of the Divine Law and Revelation *bilā kaif*—without asking how. It denies all secondary causes and prefers to call even God the Author, rather than the First Cause. There are no necessary consequences and no natural laws or causes. Lack of food does not *necessarily* cause hunger, but merely habitually accompanies it. All proceeds directly from the will of God who has established certain habits of succession or concomitance. Every event in every atom of time is the result of a direct and individual act of creation.

This final and deliberate rejection of all causality, once generally accepted, marked the end of free speculation and research, both in philosophy and in the natural sciences and frustrated the promising development of Arab historiography. It fitted well the needs of an Islamic society in which the freer social and economic life of a great commercial age was giving way to a static feudalism that was not to change for many centuries. The old conflict of conceptions smouldered on, but this new version of Islam was not seriously challenged for a thousand years, until the impact of the West in the nineteenth and twentieth centuries threatened the whole traditional structure of Islamic society and the modes of thought that were its intellectual counterpart.

IX

THE ARABS IN ECLIPSE

"*Now Turks and Tartars shake their swords at thee,*
Meaning to mangle all thy provinces."
(Marlowe, *Tamberlane the Great*, Part II)

By the eleventh century the world of Islam was in a state of manifest decay. The signs of decadence are visible even earlier, first in the political break-up, involving the loss of the authority of the central government in the remoter provinces, then in all but Iraq itself, finally in the degradation of the Caliphs to the status of mere puppets of their ministers and military commanders. In 945, the decline of the Caliphate went a step further. In that year the Buwaihids, a Persian local dynasty, advanced into Iraq and seized the capital. For the next century, the Buwaihid princes were the real rulers of the capital, assuming the title king as token of secular sovereignty. Though Shī'ites, they retained the 'Abbāsid Caliphs as figureheads and as the legal source of the sovereignty of the central government over the provinces. It is perhaps significant that not long before the first moderate Shī'ite dynasty won power, the twelfth Imām pretender of the sect disappeared into eschatological concealment. The Buwaihids restored for a while the order and prosperity of the central provinces. But the signs of economic decay were increasing. The profitable trade with China dwindled and died away, partly for reasons arising from the internal conditions of that country itself. The trade with Russia and the north diminished and disappeared during the eleventh century, while the growing shortage of precious metals helped to stifle the economic life of what was ceasing to be a commercial empire.

One of the primary causes of economic decline was undoubtedly the extravagance and lack of organisation at the centre. The lavish expenditure of the court and the inflated bureaucracy—at times maintained in duplicate in the trains of contenders for power—were not met by any great technological progress or greater development of resources. Soon the shortage of ready money forced rulers to pay senior officials and generals by farming out state revenues to them. Before long, provincial governors were appointed as tax-farmers for the areas they administered, with the duty of maintaining the local forces and officials and remitting an agreed sum to the central treasury. These governors soon became the virtually independent rulers of their provinces, rendering purely legal homage to the Caliph, whose function was reduced to giving formal, and to an increasing extent *post facto*, authorisation to their tenure of authority. The need to give the requisite military strength to governors and tax-farmers led to the practice of appointing army officers to the tax-farms and this in turn to the break-up of civil and beaucratic government and its replacement by military autocrats governing through their guards.

By the eleventh century, the weakness of the Empire was revealed by a series of almost simultaneous attacks by internal and external barbarians on all sides. In Europe, the Christian forces advanced in both Spain and Sicily, wresting great territories from Muslim rule in a wave of reconquest which culminated in the arrival of the Crusaders in the Near East itself at the end of the century. In Africa, a new religious movement among the Berbers of southern Morocco and the Senegal-Niger area led to the creation of a new Berber Empire, formed by the conquest of the greater part of north-west Africa and of those parts of Spain which had remained under Muslim rule. Further east the two great Arab Bedouin tribes of Hilāl and Sulaim burst out of the areas of Upper Egypt where they had hitherto been living and swept across Libya and Tunisia, working havoc and devastation. By 1056–57 they were able to sack the ancient Tunisian capital of Qairawān. It is to this invasion rather than to the first Arab invasion of the seventh century that the devastation and backwardness of North Africa are to be attributed. The fourteenth-century Arab historian Ibn Khaldūn, contemplating the ruin of his native land by these nomadic invasions, elaborated what was probably the first philosophy of history in terms of the cyclic interplay of the Desert and the Sown. Of these invasions he remarks: "In Tunisia and the West, since the Hilāl and Sulaim tribes passed that way at the beginning of the fifth century (the middle of the eleventh century A.D.) and devastated these countries, for three hundred and fifty years all the plains were ruined; whereas formerly from the Negro-lands to the Mediterranean all was cultivated, as is proved by the traces remaining there of monuments, buildings, farms and villages."

From Central Asia came another wave of invaders, which, in its permanent effects, was the most important of all. The Arabs had first met the Turks in central Asia and had for some time imported them to the Muslim Near East as slaves, especially of the type trained from early childhood for military and administrative purposes and later known as *Mamlūk* (owned), to distinguish them from the humbler slaves used for domestic and other purposes. We find occasional Turkish slaves under the early 'Abbāsids and even under the Umayyads, but the first to use them extensively was Mu'taṣim (833–842), who collected a large force of Turkish military slaves even before his accession, and later arranged to receive a large number annually as part of the tribute from the eastern provinces. The old Khurāsānī guards of the 'Abbāsid Caliphs had become Arabised and identified with the local population. The Persian aristocracy had now found its own political outlet in the independent dynasties of Iran, and so the Caliphs found it necessary to seek a new basis of support. They found it in the Turkish Mamlūks under their Turkish commanders, expatriates with no local, tribal, family, national or religious affiliations, therefore the more devoted to the central government. From the beginning the Turks were noted for their superior military qualities, which seem to have lain mainly in their use of mounted bowmen and the nomadic speed of their cavalry. From this time on the Caliphs relied to an increasing extent on Turkish troops and commanders, to the detriment of the older cultured peoples in Islam, the Arabs and the Persians. The progressive militarisation of the regime increased their strength.

By the eleventh century the Turks were entering the world of Islam, not only as individuals recruited by capture or purchase, but by the migration of whole tribes of free nomadic Turks still organised in their own traditional way. The consolidation of the Sung regime in China after an interregnum of disorder cut off the route of expansion into China and forced the Central Asian nomads to expand westwards. These Turkish invaders of Islam belong to the Oghuz tribes and are usually known as Seljuqs, after the name of the military family that led them.

The Seljuqs entered the territories of the Caliphate *ca.* 970, and soon accepted Islam. Within a short time they had conquered the greater part of Persia, and in 1055 Tughrul Bey entered Baghdad, defeating the Buwaihids and incorporating Iraq in the Seljuq realm. In a few years the Seljuqs had wrested Syria and Palestine from the local rulers and from the declining Fāṭimids and, succeeding where the Arabs had formerly failed, conquered from the Byzantines a great part of Anatolia which became and remained a Muslim and Turkish land.

The Seljuqs were Sunnī Muslims, and their capture of the city of Baghdad was regarded by many as a liberation from the heretical Buwaihids. The Caliphs remained as nominal rulers, but the real sovereigns of the Empire, the greater part of which was now united under a single authority for the first time since the early Caliphate, were the Seljuq Grand Sultans, who defeated both the Byzantines and the Fāṭimids in the west.

The new rulers of the Empire relied largely in administration on Persians and on the Persian bureaucracy. One of the most notable figures of the age was the great Persian minister Niẓām al-Mulk, who developed and systematised the trend towards feudalism that was already inherent in the tax-farming practices of the immediately preceding period. The misuses of the previous era became the rules of a new social and administrative order based on land instead of money. Land was granted to or taken by officers. In return they furnished a number of armed men. These grants carried rights not merely to a commission on the collection of taxes, but to the revenues themselves. Though occasionally they became hereditary by usurpation, in theory and in usual practice they were granted only for a term of years, and were always revocable. The historian 'Imād ad-Dīn, writing in the Seljuq period, points out that this was the only way to give the turbulent Turkish tribesmen and soldiery an interest in the prosperity of agriculture and remarks: "It had been the custom to collect money from the country and pay it to the troops and no one had previously had a fief. Niẓām al-Mulk saw that the money was not coming in from the country on account of its disturbed state and that the yield was uncertain because of its disorder. Therefore he divided it among the troops in fiefs, assigning to them both the yield and the revenue. Their interest in its development increased greatly and it returned rapidly to a flourishing state." In these few simple words he has described the long transition from a monetary to a feudal economy.

Social upheavals in such a period of change were inevitable. Landowners under the old regime were hard hit by the rise of a new class of non-resident feudal lords. Trade withered and declined. Perhaps the clearest indication of the decline of trade is to be found in the coin hoards of Scandinavia. During the ninth and tenth centuries Arabic and Persian coins are very numerous and indeed predominate in these hoards. During the eleventh century they decrease greatly in numbers; thereafter they disappear. The chief opposition movement in this period was again the Ismā'īlīs, but in a new and changed form. In 1078 Ḥasan-i Ṣabbāḥ, a Persian Ismā'īlī leader, visited the Fāṭimid capital of Cairo. There he came into conflict with the military autocrat who was the real ruler of the Fāṭimid realms in the name of the decaying Imāms. On the death of the Fāṭimid Caliph Mustanṣir in 1094, Ḥasan-i Ṣabbāḥ and his Persian followers refused to recognise the successor nominated for his tameness by the military ruler, and severed connections with the emasculated organisation in Cairo. The eastern Ismā'īlīs now proclaimed their allegiance to Nizār, an elder son of Mustanṣir who had been passed over in the succession, and embarked on a new period of intense activity as an illegal revolutionary movement in the Seljuq dominions. The followers of the "New Preaching", as the reformed Ismā'īlism of Ḥasan-i Ṣabbāḥ is known, are usually called Assassins, from the Arabic *hashīshī*, possibly in reference to the means by which they were alleged to have induced ecstasy in the faithful. The European meaning of the word derives from the political tactics of the sect.

In 1090 Ḥasan-i Ṣabbāḥ obtained control of the inaccessible mountain fastness of Alamūt in northern Persia. Here, and in similar bases established in Syria in the following century, the "Old Man of the Mountain", as the Grand Masters of the sect were called, commanded bands of devoted and fanatical followers, waging a campaign of terror and 'assassination' against the kings and princes of Islam in the name of a mysterious hidden Imām. The emissaries of the Grand Masters carried out a series of daring murders of prominent Muslim statesmen and generals, including the Niẓām al-Mulk himself, in 1092. The Western chroniclers of the Crusades depict vividly the fear which they inspired in Syria among Muslims and Crusaders alike, and made their name known and feared even in Europe. The terror of the assassins was not finally exorcised until the Mongol invasions of the thirteenth century, after which Ismā'īlism stagnated as a minor heresy.

The economic reorganisation of the early Seljuq period had its counterpart in religious life. In Baghdad and elsewhere religious colleges, known as *Madrasa*, were founded, which became the pattern of the many others that followed in the Islamic world. The Niẓāmīya of Baghdad, named after the great minister who founded it, and its sisters were centres of orthodoxy, more especially of the revived traditionalism now becoming general, and were intended to a large extent to counter the revolutionary heterodoxy of the Ismā'īlīs and the intellectual radicalism of the preceding period. Al-Ghazālī (1059–1111), one of the greatest of Muslim religious thinkers, taught here for a while. His works include refutations both of philosophy and of heresy.

After the death of the Niẓām al-Mulk the political fragmentation of the Near and Middle East was resumed. The Seljuq Empire broke up into a series of smaller succession states ruled by members or officers of the Seljuq House. It was during this period of weakness that in 1096 the Crusaders arrived in the Near East. Despite the idealistic aspect of this great movement, best exemplified in the ill-starred Crusade of the Children, in the perspective of the Near East the Crusades were essentially an early experiment in expansionist imperialism, motivated by material considerations with religion as a psychological catalyst. Traders from the Italian city republics following the trade they had established with Byzantium and the Fāṭimids to the sources of supply, warlike and ambitous barons, younger sons in search of principalities and sinners in search of profitable penance—these rather than the seekers of the Holy Sepulchre were the significant and characteristic figures of the invasion from the West.

For the first thirty years the disunity of the Muslim world made things easy for the invaders, who advanced rapidly down the coast of Syria into Palestine, establishing a chain of Latin feudal principalities, based on Antioch, Edessa, Tripoli and Jerusalem. This first period was one of colonisation and assimilation. Conquerors and pilgrims settled in Syria, adopting local dress and customs, intermarrying with the local Christians. Fulcher of Chartres, a chronicler of the First Crusade, remarks:

> "Now we who were westerners have become easterners. He who was Italian or French has in this land become a Galilean or a Palestinean. He who was a citizen of Rheims or Chartres is now a Tyrian or an Antiochene. We have already forgotten our birthplaces. Most of us do not know them or even hear of them. One already owns home and household as if by paternal and hereditary right, another has taken as wife not a compatriot, but a Syrian, Armenian, or even a baptised Saracen woman. . . . He who was an alien has become a native, he who was immigrant is now a resident. Every day our relations and friends follow us, willingly abandoning whatever they possessed in the West. For those who were poor there, has God made rich here. Those

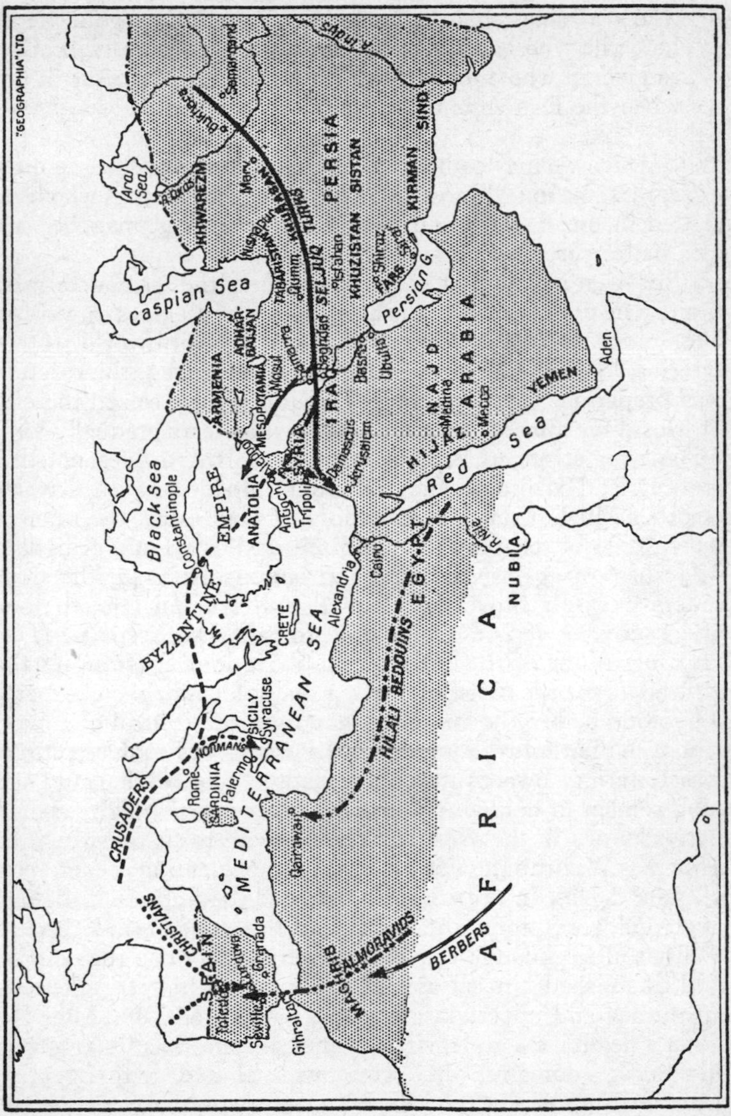

The great invasions of the eleventh century

> who had a few pence there, have numberless gold pieces here; he who had not a village there possesses, with God as giver, a whole town here. Why then return to the West, when the East suits us so well?"

With which we may compare the remark of the twelfth-century Syrian Usāma ibn Munqidh: "There are some Franks who have settled in our country and lived among the Muslims: they are of a better sort than those who have come recently. . . ."

But even in this first period of success the Crusaders were limited in the main to the coastal plains and slopes, always in close touch with the Mediterranean and Western world. In the interior, looking eastwards to the desert and Iraq, the reaction was preparing. In 1127 Zangī, a Seljuq officer, seized the city of Mosul for himself, and in the following years gradually built up an ever stronger Muslim state in northern Mesopotamia and Syria. His progress was at first impeded by the rivalry of other Muslim states and notably of Damascus, the ruler of which did not scruple to ally himself with the Latin Kingdom of Jerusalem against the common enemy. In 1147, the Crusaders unwisely broke the alliance, and Nūr ad-Dīn, the son and successor of Zangī, was able to take Damascus in 1154, creating a single Muslim state in Syria and confronting the Crusaders for the first time with a really formidable adversary. The issue before the two sides now was the control of Egypt, where the Fāṭimid Caliphate, in the last stages of decrepitude, was tottering towards its final collapse. The result could not long remain in doubt. A Kurdish officer called Ṣalāḥ ad-Dīn better known in the West as Saladin, went to Egypt, where he served as Wazīr to the Fāṭimids while representing the interests of Nūr ad-Dīn. In 1171 Saladin declared the Fāṭimid Caliphate at an end. He restored the mention of the name of the 'Abbāsid Caliphs of Baghdad in the Mosque services and on the coinage and established himself as effective ruler of Egypt, professing an uneasy and uncertain allegiance to Nūr ad-Dīn. After the latter's death in 1174, leaving a minor as heir, Saladin absorbed his Syrian domains, thus creating a united Syro-Egyptian Muslim Empire. In 1187 he felt strong enough to attack the

Crusaders. By his death in 1193 he had recaptured Jerusalem and expelled them from all but a narrow coastal strip which they held from the towns of Acre, Tyre, Tripoli and Antioch.

The united Syro-Egyptian state created by Saladin did not last long. Under his successors, the Ayyūbids, Syria broke up once again into a number of small states, but Egypt remained a strong united monarchy, the chief Muslim power in the Near East and the main bulwark of Islam against the West, defeating the repeated attempts of the later Crusades to recapture the Holy Land.

The chief permanent effect of the Crusades in the Near East was in trade. Colonies of Western merchants had flourished in the Levant ports under crusading rule. They survived under the Muslim reconquest and developed a considerable trade both of export and import. In 1174, Saladin, writing to the Caliph in Baghdad, justified his encouragement of this trade. The Venetians, the Genoese, and the Pisans, he said, were bringing choice products of the West, especially arms and war material. This constituted an advantage for the Muslims and an injury for the Christians. The thunder of the church in Europe against this trade and the decrees of excommunication against those who engaged in it were ineffective.

Meanwhile a new and more dangerous threat to Islam was arising in the East. Far away in eastern Asia Jenghiz Khān had, after a bitter internal war, united the nomadic tribes of Mongolia and launched them on a career of conquest which in extent must rank as one of the most remarkable in human history. By 1220 the Mongols had conquered all Transoxania. In 1221 Jenghiz crossed the Oxus river and entered Persia. His death in 1227 was followed by a pause, but in the middle of the century a new move westward was planned and executed. The Mongol Prince Hülekü crossed the Oxus river with instructions from the Great Khān of Mongolia to conquer all the lands of Islam as far as Egypt. His armies swept through Persia, overcoming all resistance and crushing even the Ismā'īlīs, who had resisted all previous attacks. In 1258, Hülekü captured Baghdad, killed the Caliph and abolished the 'Abbāsid Caliphate. The destruction of this great historic institution, even in decay still the legal centre of Islam and the token of its unity, was the end of an era in Islamic history. Yet in some ways the shock was perhaps not as great as is sometimes suggested. The Caliphs had long since lost almost all their real power, and secular Sulṭāns, both in the capital and in the provinces, had begun to arrogate to themselves not only the powers, but even some of the prerogatives, of the Caliphs. The Mongols did little more than lay the ghost of an institution that was already dead.

Unlike the Seljuqs, the Mongol invaders were still heathens and showed no interest in Islam, its traditions and its institutions. The destruction which they wrought in the lands they conquered has been much exaggerated. Most of it was purely strategic, not wilful. It ceased after the campaigns of conquest of which it was a part, and in Persia under Mongol rule a new period of economic and cultural development began. But in Iraq the immediate effects of the Mongol conquests were the breakdown of civil government and the collapse of the irrigation works on which the country depended, aggravated by the inroads of Bedouin tribes once the control of the sedentary power was relaxed.

Still more fatal for the prosperity of Iraq was its inclusion, as an outlying province, in an eastern empire the centre of which lay in Persia. Henceforth the valley of the Tigris and the Euphrates, cut off from the Mediterranean provinces in the west by a frontier of sand and steel, outflanked in the east by the rise of the Persian centre to which it was subordinated, could no longer serve as channel for the East-West trade, which moved north and east to Turkey and Persia, westward to Egypt and the Red Sea, leaving Iraq and the fallen city of the Caliphs to centuries of stagnation and neglect.

Despite some raids into Syria, the direct effects of the Mongol conquest on the Arab world were confined to Iraq, which was now attached to the Mongol State centred on Persia. Syria and Egypt were saved from the Mongols by the new regime that had grown out of the Ayyūbid monarchy. Though the Ayyūbids themselves were Kurds in origin, their regime was of Turkish Seljuq type. The ruling class was a military autocracy of Turkish pretorians, often able to control the Ayyūbid Sulṭān himself.

In the middle of the thirteenth century the power of the Turkish Mamlūks in Cairo was supreme and a new regime emerged, the Mamlūk Sultanate, which ruled Egypt and Syria until 1517. In 1260, after a period of confusion following the death of the last Ayyūbid, a Qipchaq Turk called Baibars became Sultan. His career in many ways forms an interesting parallel with that of Saladin. He united Muslim Syria and Egypt into a single state, this time more permanently. He defeated the external enemies of that state, repulsing Mongol invaders from the east and crushing all but the last remnants of the Crusaders in Syria. An idea of genius was to invite a member of the 'Abbāsid family to establish himself in Cairo with the title of Caliph. The line of 'Abbāsid Caliphs in Cairo were mere court functionaries of the Mamlūk Sulṭāns. The Egyptian historian Maqrīzī (*d.* 1442), remarks: "The Turkish Mamlūks installed as Caliph a man to whom they gave the name and titles of Caliph. He had no authority and no right to express his opinion. He passed his time with the commanders, the great officers, the officials and the judges, visiting them to thank them for the dinners and parties to which they had invited him." The Cairo Caliphs represent the final stage in the decay of the Caliphate.

The Mamlūk system of Baibars and his successors was feudal and was an adaptation of the Seljuq feudalism brought into Syria and Egypt by the Ayyūbids. An officer or amīr received a grant of land in lieu of pay and on condition of maintaining a certain number of Mamlūk soldiers, varying between five and a hundred according to his rank. He normally devoted two-thirds of his revenues to their upkeep. The grants were not hereditary though there were many attempts to make them so. The system was based on the permanent eviction of the Arabised descendants of the Mamlūk officers by newly imported Mamlūks, thus preventing, perhaps deliberately, the formation of a hereditary landed aristocracy. A Mamlūk officer received his grant for life or less. He did not normally reside on his estates, but in Cairo or in the chief town of the district where his fief lay. He was interested in revenue rather than possession. The system therefore developed no *châteaux* or manors or strong local authorities of the Western type. There was no subinfeudation, and even the division of the land in Egypt into fiefs was not permanent, being subject to a periodic territorial refount.

The Mamlūks themselves were bought slaves, trained and educated in Egypt. At first they were mainly Qipchaq Turks from the northern shores of the Black Sea, later they included Mongol deserters and men of other races, chiefly Circassians, with occasional Greeks, Kurds, and even some Europeans. But Turkish or Circassian remained the language of the dominant class, many of whom, including some Sultans, could hardly speak Arabic. The Mamlūk state as developed by Baibars and his successors was based on a highly elaborate dual administration, civil and military, both sides controlled by Mamlūk officers with civilian staffs. Until 1383 the Mamlūk Sultans followed one another in more or less hereditary succession. Thereafter the Sultanate was held by the strongest commander. On the death of a Sultan his son succeeded as formal head during an interregnum while the real succession was decided.

In the first period the Mamlūks were threatened by Christian and Mongol enemies, and their supreme achievement is their defence of the Islamic civilisation of the Near East against these enemies. During the fifteenth century a new power arose—the Ottoman Empire, rising like a phoenix from the ruins of the Seljuq Sultanate of Anatolia. Relations between the two states were at first friendly, but conflicts arose when the Ottomans, safely established in Europe, turned their attention to Asia.

The trade with Europe, and particularly the trade between Europe and the Further East via the Near East, was of vital importance to Egypt, both for the trade itself and for the customs revenues derived from it. During periods of strength Mamlūk governments protected and encouraged this trade, which brought Egypt great prosperity and a new flowering of arts and letters. But the Mongol threat, warded off by Baibars, was not yet averted. In 1400–1401 the Turco-Mongol forces of Tīmūr (Tamerlane) ravaged Syria and sacked Damascus. Plague, locusts and the depredations of the unleashed Bedouin completed the work of the departed Mongols, and the Mamlūk Sultanate suffered a blow to its economic and military strength from which it never recovered.

The crises of the fifteenth century brought new fiscal policies aimed at extracting the maximum profit from the transit trade. After first encouraging Indian and even Chinese merchants to bring their wares to ports under Egyptian control, Sultan Barsbay (1422–1438) had the idea that it might be even better to seize the trade than to tax it. He began by making sugar a royal monopoly, and followed it with pepper and other commodities. These policies, maintained by his successors, led to rising prices, foreign reprisals, and ultimately to general economic collapse, in which the government could survive only by currency depreciation and by drastic and violent taxation.

The historians of the period paint a vivid picture of the increasing corruption and inefficiency of the regime in its last days. One historian, speaking of the Wazīrs, remarks: "They were cruel rascals, inventors of a thousand injustices, arrogant and presumptuous. They were famous neither for their knowledge nor for their religious spirit. They were the scourges of their age, always with a causeless insult ready in their mouths. Their existence, passed exclusively in oppressing the people of their time, was a disgrace to humanity." When Sultan Barsbay convened the four chief Qāḍīs of Cairo and asked them to authorise new taxes over and above those laid down by the Holy Law, one of them was reputed to have replied: "How can we authorise the taking of money from the Muslims when a wife of the Sultan wore on the day of her son's circumcision a dress worth 30,000 dinars; and that is only one dress and only one wife."

In 1498 came the crowning catastrophe. On May 17th of that year the Portuguese navigator Vasco da Gama landed in India, having come by sea round the Cape of Good Hope. In August 1499 he returned to Lisbon with a cargo of spices. He had opened a new route from Europe to the Further East, cheaper and safer than the old one. Other expeditions followed rapidly.

The Portuguese established bases in India, and developed direct trade, dealing a mortal blow to the Egyptian route and cutting off the very lifeblood of the Mamlūk state. The Mamlūks, recognising the immediate consequences of these events, and urged to action by their Venetian fellow-sufferers from this diversion, tried by diplomacy and then by war to avert the Portuguese menace. Their efforts were fruitless. The Portuguese fleets, built to face the Atlantic gales, were superior in structure, armament and navigational skill to those of the Muslims. Soon they were able to defeat the Egyptian squadrons, systematically destroy Arab merchant shipping in the Indian Ocean, and penetrate even to the Persian Gulf and the Red Sea. In the sixteenth century, after the Ottoman conquest and the growth of European commercial enterprise, the Levant trade revived to some extent, but remained of secondary importance. The Arab Near East had been outflanked. Not until the nineteenth century did the main routes of world trade return to it.

During the long period that we have been considering three significant changes emerge. The first of these is the transformation of the Islamic Near East from a commercial monetary economy to one which, despite an extensive and important foreign and transit trade, was internally a feudal economy, based on subsistence agriculture. The second is the end of the political independence of the sedentary Arabs and Arabic-speaking people and their replacement by the Turks. In the vast but thinly peopled deserts the Arab tribes retained the independence they had recovered during the decay of the 'Abbāsids, defying repeated attempts to impose control over them and often eroding the frontiers of the cultivated land in their long struggle with the Turks. In a few mountain outposts, too, men who spoke Arabic retained their independence. But everywhere else, in the cities and in the cultivated valleys and plains of Iraq, Syria and Egypt, for a thousand years people of Arabic speech were no longer to rule themselves. So deep-rooted was the feeling that only the Turks were equipped by nature to govern that in the fourteenth century we find a Mamlūk secretary of Syrian birth addressing the Arabs in

Turkish through an interpreter rather than in his mother-tongue, for fear lest he should lose face by speaking the despised language of the subject people. As late as the beginning of the nineteenth century Napoleon, when he invaded Egypt, tried unsuccessfully to appoint Arabic-speaking Egyptians to positions of authority and was forced to resort to Turks who alone could command obedience.

The third change is the shifting of the centre of gravity of the Arabic-speaking world from Iraq to Egypt. The disorganisation and weakness of Iraq and its remoteness from the Mediterranean, across which both the traders and the enemies of the later period were to come, ruled that country out as a possible base. The only alternative was Egypt, the other trade-route, and the irrigated valley of a single river, which by its very nature demanded a single centralised government—the only powerful centralised state in the Arab Near East.

With the power of the Arabs went the glory. The Persian and Turkish-speaking rulers who inherited the thrones of the Arabs patronised poets who could praise them in their own languages, according to their own tastes and traditions. First the Persians then the Turks developed independent Muslim culture languages of their own, and, with the political leadership, assumed the cultural leadership of Islam. Under Seljuq and Mongol rule the Islamic arts entered new periods of efflorescence. Both Persian and Turkish literatures, while strongly coloured by the Arab-Islamic tradition, branched out on independent and significant lines. After Seljuq times the literary use of Arabic was confined to the Arabic-speaking countries, except for a limited output of theological and scientific works. The movement of the centre of gravity of the Arab world westwards gave greater importance to Syria, and still more to Egypt, which now became the main centres of Arabic culture.

The development of a static society and the predominance of a static formalist theology led to a decline in independent speculation and research. The passive dependence on authority in public life found its parallel in literature, which suffered a loss of vitality and independence. The most striking feature of the time is the increased stress on form for artists, on memory for scholars. But there were still some great figures—Ghazālī (1059–1111), one of the greatest thinkers of Islam, who attempted to combine the new scholasticism with the intuitive and mystical religion of the Sūfīs; Ḥarīrī (1054–1122), still regarded by the Arabic-speaking peoples as the supreme exponent of literary form and elegance; Yāqūt (1179–1229), biographer, geographer and scholar, and in post-Mongol times a series of historians or rather historical compilers, among whom the Tunisian Ibn Khaldūn (1332–1406) stands alone as the greatest historical genius of Islam and the first to produce a philosophic and sociological conception of history.

In 1517 the weakened and decaying Mamlūk Empire crumbled before the Ottoman assault and for four hundred years Syria and Egypt formed part of the Ottoman Empire. Soon the Barbary States as far as the frontiers of Morocco accepted Ottoman suzerainty, and with the final Ottoman conquest of Iraq from Persia in 1639, almost the whole Arabic-speaking world was under Ottoman rule.

Only in a few places did the peoples of Arabic speech retain any real independence. In Arabia, the south-western province of Yemen became an Ottoman Pashalik in 1537, but recovered its independence in 1635. The Arab rulers of Mecca and the Ḥijāz, the Sharīfs, recognised Ottoman suzerainty and were dependent on Cairo rather than on Constantinople. For the rest the Bedouin of the Peninsula maintained their independence in the inhospitable deserts. In the mid-eighteenth century they produced a potent spiritual movement, in some ways resembling the rise of Islam itself. A jurist of Najd called Muḥammad ibn 'Abd al-Wahhāb (1703–1791) founded a new sect, based on a rigid, anti-mystical puritanism. In the name of the pure, primitive Islam of the first century, he denounced all subsequent accretions of belief and ritual as superstitious "innovation", alien to true Islam. He forbade the worship of holy men and holy places, even the exaggerated veneration of Muḥammad, and rejected all forms of mediation. He applied the same puritan austerity to religious and personal life. The conversion to the Wahhābī doctrine of the Najdī amīr Muḥammad ibn Su'ūd gave the sect a military and political focus. Soon Wahhābism spread by conquest over most of central Arabia, wresting the holy cities of Mecca and Medina from the Sharīfs who ruled them in the Ottoman name and threatening even the Ottoman provinces of Syria and Iraq. The reaction came in 1818, when an invading Turco-Egyptian army sent by Muḥammad 'Alī, the pasha of Egypt, broke the power of the Wahhābī empire and confined Wahhābism to its native Najd. There the sect survived with somewhat diminished vigour, to reappear as a political factor in the mid-nineteenth and again in the twentieth century.

In the Lebanon a tradition of independence in the mountain areas had existed from early times, when Christian invaders from Anatolia turned the upper reaches of the mountain into a Christian island among the surrounding sea of Islam. Semi-independent local dynasties, some Christian, some Muslim, some Druse, continued to rule parts of the mountain under Ottoman suzerainty, with a degree of independence that varied with the efficacy of Ottoman government. Finally, in the Far West the mixed Arab-Berber Empire of Morocco retained its independence and developed along lines peculiarly its own.

For the rest, the subjection of the Arabs to Turkish rule, begun under the Caliph Mu'taṣim, confirmed by the Seljuqs and Mamlūks, was maintained by the Ottomans. Such movements of independence as there were in the Arab provinces were organised more often than not by rebellious Turkish Pashas rather than by any local leaders.

In Egypt the Ottomans maintained the Mamlūk order, superimposing an Ottoman Pasha and garrison upon it. But the feudal system lost its military character and came to be based on revenue rather than on military service. Most of the fiefs became *Iltizām*—usufructuary assignments of state lands to officials and others with limited rights of succession and disposal. The assignee collected annual payments from non-owning peasants. Both the assignee (*Multazim*) and the peasant paid taxes. The Multazim's heirs could succeed on payment of a due. With the weakening of central control the local Beys seized power and the Pasha became a passive observer of their rivalries. Sometimes they were able to win full control.

The Ottoman conquest brought a greater degree of change to Syria. In the early seventeenth century the country was divided into the three Ottoman Pashaliks of Damascus, Aleppo, and Tripoli, to which a fourth, Saida, was added in 1660. Each was under a Pasha who bought his post and enjoyed a large measure of local freedom of action, varying according to circumstances and personality. The Pashaliks themselves were organised on Ottoman feudal lines. Most of the land was divided among fief-holders, mainly Turks. The fiefs were semi-hereditary and carried the obligation of paying annual dues and rendering military service with retainers. The rights of the fief-holder were the collection of taxes and the exercise of some seigneurial powers over the peasantry. Many Iltizāms of crown lands were held by court dignitaries in Constantinople. The Pashas had great powers, increasing with the distance from the capital and the weakness of the government.

At first the Ottoman conquest was an advantage, bringing relative security and prosperity after the heady nightmare of late Mamlūk rule. But by the eighteenth century the decline of the Ottoman Empire brought general misrule and corruption, anarchy and stagnation. During this long period of alien rule, this mutually disadvantageous association of two cultures, each perforce entangled in the other's decline, the spirit of revolt is still discernible. The Ismā'īlī movement had dwindled into insignificance after the Mongol invasions, but other movements replaced it. Even under the Mamlūks there were sporadic revolts of the Arabic-speaking Egyptian population. Occasional movements for independence under the Ottomans were usually due to ambitious individuals, often themselves Turkish governors. The really popular opposition, in accordance with Islamic tradition, was expressed religiously, this time in Sūfism. This was at first a purely individual mystical experience, then a social movement with an extensive following among the lower orders, organised in Dervish brotherhoods, often associated with craft guilds. The Sūfīs were not formally heretical as the Ismāʿīlīs had been, and were politically quietist. In religion they opposed a personal mystic faith to the dominant orthodox transcendentalism which at times they succeeded in influencing. As far as they had any direct political expression, it was hostile to the existing order. But the Sūfī revolt by infiltration failed just as the head-on Ismāʿīlī assault had failed in its time. The static elements were too strong. Real change was to come from a new factor from outside, more powerful and infinitely more aggressive than the Hellenistic impulses that had quickened the intellectual ferment of mediaeval Islam.

X

THE IMPACT OF THE WEST

"Icci, beatis nunc Arabum invides
gazis, et acrem militiam paras
non ante devictis Sabaeae
regibus, horribilique Medo
nectis catenas?"

(Horace: Odes I, 29)

THE Arabs had been in contact with western Europe since the time of the first conquests. In Spain and Sicily they had ruled western European populations and had maintained military, diplomatic and commercial relations with other western European states. They had received west European students in their universities. The Crusaders had brought a piece of western Europe to the very heart of the Arab East. But these contacts, fruitful for the West which had learnt much from the Arabs, had little effect on the latter. For them the relations were and remained external and superficial and had but little influence on Arab life and culture. The geographical and historical literature of the mediaeval Arabs reflects their complete lack of interest in western Europe, which they regarded as an outer darkness of barbarism from which the sunlit world of Islam had little to fear and less to learn. "The peoples of the north," says the tenth-century geographer Mas'ūdī, "are those for whom the sun is distant from the Zenith . . . cold and damp prevail in those regions, and snow and ice follow one another in endless succession. The warm humour is lacking among them; their bodies are large, their natures gross, their manners harsh, their understanding dull and their tongues heavy . . . their religious beliefs lack solidity . . . those of them who are farthest to the north are the most subject to stupidity, grossness and brutishness." An eleventh-century Qāḍī of Toledo, in a work on the nations who have cultivated knowledge, enumerates the Indians, Persians, Chaldees, Greeks, Romans (including Byzantines and eastern Christians), Egyptians, Arabs and Jews. Among the rest, he singles out the Chinese and the Turks as "noble peoples" who have distinguished themselves in other fields, and contemptuously dismisses the remainder as the northern and southern barbarians, remarking of the former: "Their bellies are big, their colour pale, their hair long and lank. They lack keenness of understanding and clarity of intelligence, and are overcome by ignorance and foolishness, blindness and stupidity." As late as the fourteenth century no less a man than Ibn Khaldūn could still remark dubiously: "We have heard of late that in the lands of the Franks, that is, the country of Rome and its dependencies on the northern shore of the Mediterranean, the philosophic sciences flourish . . . and their students are plentiful. But God knows best what goes on in those parts." This attitude was at first justified, but with the progress of western Europe it became dangerously out of date.

From the beginning of the sixteenth century a new relationship between Islam and the West is discernible. The West had made great technological advances in the crafts of war and peace. It had renewed itself through the Renaissance and the Reformation. The break-up of the feudal order had freed trade and unleashed enterprise, for which the consolidation of centralised nation states provided solid and reliable political instruments, and so began the great expansion of western Europe which by the twentieth century had forced the whole world into its economic, political and cultural orbit.

In the Near East the imposing outward strength of the Ottoman Empire concealed the deep weaknesses of a military autocracy with a decaying social order. The moral bond of religious unity was of diminishing effectiveness. Corruption and disorder in government and a decline in standards were aggravated by economic backwardness. Neither the military ruling class nor the intellectual class were interested in economic change.

European expansion at the beginning of the sixteenth century was of a new type. It began with French negotiations with the Ottomans for an alliance against a common enemy. Skilful diplomacy transformed that alliance into a trade pact, giving certain rights and privileges to French traders in the Ottoman territories. These rights were enshrined in the so-called Capitulations of 1535, guaranteeing to French traders the safety of their persons and property, freedom of worship, etc. This was in effect a measure of extra-territoriality. It was at first not a concession wrung from a weak oriental Power, but the granting, by a gesture almost of condescension, of the rights of Dhimmīs in Muslim society, extended by the inner logic of the Muslim code to foreign Christians.

French penetration developed rapidly. French traders took advantage of the opportunities they had won to establish trading posts and consular missions in both Syria and Egypt. Other Capitulations followed later, to the English (1580), the Dutch (1612), and other powers. During the seventeenth and the eighteenth centuries European trade grew steadily and numerous colonies of traders settled in the ports and other towns of Syria and Egypt under the protection of their consuls.

Until the nineteenth century, the military, as distinct from the commercial, advance of Europe in the Near and Middle Eastern Muslim world was limited to its northern borders, where Austria and Russia advanced steadily at the Ottoman expense into the Balkans and along the northern and eastern shores of the Black Sea. The Arab lands were affected only commercially, mainly by English, French and Italian traders, who came to buy and sell. A great change came with the occupation of Egypt in 1798 by Napoleon Buonaparte. This expedition, the first armed inroad of Europe on the Arab Near East since the Crusades, began a new era. The Ottoman Mamlūk order crumbled at once and the French were able to occupy the country without serious difficulty. Their rule in Egypt was of brief duration but profound significance. It began the period of direct Western intervention in the Arab world, with great economic and social consequences. By the easy victory which they won the French shattered the illusion of the unchallengeable superiority of the Islamic world to the infidel

West, thus posing a profound problem of readjustment to a new relationship. The psychological disorders thus engendered have not yet been resolved.

The period of anarchy that followed the French withdrawal ended with the emergence of Muḥammad 'Alī, an Ottoman soldier of Balkan origin, who succeeded in making himself virtually independent ruler of Egypt and for a short time of Arabia and Syria also, until confined to Egypt once more by the Western Powers.

Muḥammad 'Alī's efforts at independence and expansion were frustrated by the Great Powers. He succeeded only in establishing a hereditary governorship of an autonomous Ottoman province of Egypt, but he began a great programme of reforms. They were military in origin, deriving from the desire to have a new European-type army. To achieve this, he initiated an ambitious programme of economic and educational measures. The former were particularly successful. His project of industrialisation failed, but he began to break up the legal feudal order in Egypt and Syria, and rationalised and extended agriculture. In education he opened new schools with Western teachers, sponsored translations of Western books which he printed in a press set up for the purpose in Cairo, and sent student missions to Europe, the first of a long series. The extension of cotton cultivation in Egypt under Muḥammad 'Alī and his successors led to closer economic links with western Europe and especially with England, the main market for Egyptian cotton. The spread of European languages and ideas through education at home and by missions abroad subjected the traditional outlook to the impact of new ideas.

Muḥammad 'Alī himself was a Turkish-speaking Ottoman and no Arab; he had no thought of an Arab Empire based on a people whom, like most Turks of his time, he despised. But he operated in Arab countries, to which he gave a measure of political independence, and raised Egyptian and Syrian armies —and his son (or step-son) Ibrāhīm spoke Arabic and thought of an Arab Empire.

Syria returned to the Ottoman Empire after the withdrawal

of Muḥammad 'Alī's forces in 1840. But the break-up of the feudal order and its replacement by a centralised administration continued under Ottoman auspices. The Ottoman reforms brought an increased measure of centralisation. The provinces now were no longer feudal grants held by military Pashas, but administrative districts governed by salaried officials of the central government. The landowning classes, though deprived of their feudal privileges and powers in law, retained their social and economic pre-eminence and remained the dominant class in economic and administrative life.

Meanwhile, European economic activity had entered upon a new phase. Europeans were now no longer mainly concerned with trade, but with the development and control, either directly by concessions or indirectly by loans to local governments, of resources and services, and most especially of communications. Since the days of Vasco da Gama the European approach to India, whether for trade or war, had been by the open sea, round the Cape of Good Hope, rather than the Middle East. But throughout this period there had been some who had thought of a return to the ancient overland highways, and had even attempted, without success, to accomplish it. Napoleon's expedition to Egypt drew attention sharply to the possibility. The advent of the steamship, independent of the periodic winds of the eastern seas, made it a reality.

European vessels, mainly from India, had occasionally penetrated the Red Sea and Persian Gulf for centuries, bringing the produce of the Indies to the marts of Baṣra, Jedda and sometimes even Suez. From the beginning of the nineteenth century British companies from India ran regular shipping services to both Baṣra and Suez. To secure them, British Indian naval units charted the Arabian seas, put down Arabian piracy by force of arms, and at the same time acquired coaling-stations and strategic watch-points. A series of expeditions from Bombay against the predatory tribes of the eastern and south-eastern coasts of Arabia culminated in the treaty of peace of 1820 with the Gulf Sheikhs, founding a British political supremacy in the area that was strengthened in gradual stages through the century. The convenient piracy of the Sultan of

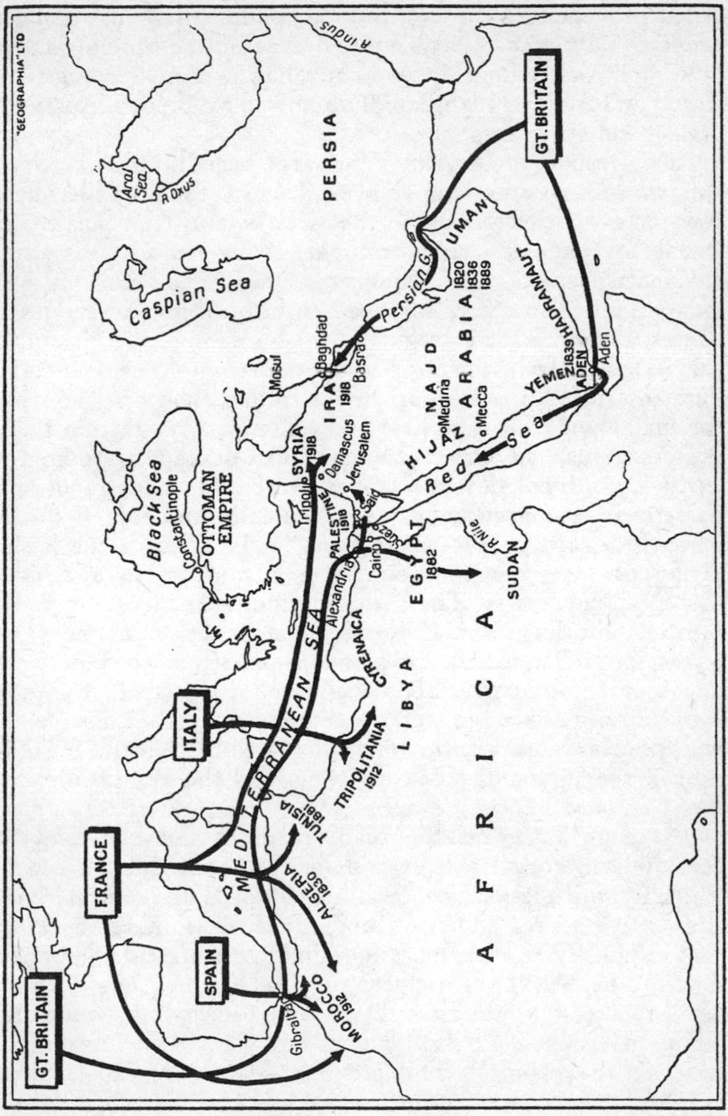

The attack of the West in the nineteenth and twentieth centuries

Aden provoked its capture and occupation in 1839, similarly securing the approaches to the Red Sea. On the Mediterranean side, a British steamship company began regular services to Egypt and Syria in 1836, rapidly followed by French, Austrian, Italian and other lines.

A corresponding development of the overland links between the two seas was not long delayed. In 1800 there was hardly a road or a wheeled vehicle in the Arab orient, transport being mainly by pack and riding animals or by inland waterways. European capital and engineers wrought a vast change. In 1834 a British officer surveyed both the Iraqi and Egyptian routes, and from 1836 a regular British steamboat service plied the rivers of Iraq, linking Mesopotamia with Baṣra and the Persian Gulf. But it was on Egypt, rather than on Iraq, that the final choice fell. The East India Company and, from 1840, the Peninsular and Oriental Steamship Company were first in the field, with an Alexandria-Suez overland link for goods and passengers, using steamboats on the Nile and inland canals and wheel-carts on the newly built roads. In 1851 the Pasha of Egypt gave George Stephenson a contract to build the first Egyptian railway. The Cairo-Alexandria line was completed in 1856, the link from Cairo to Suez in the following year. Railway development in Egypt was rapid. By 1863 there were 245 miles of track, by 1882 well over a thousand, by 1914 over 3000. The opening of the Suez Canal, after ten years' work, on November 17th, 1869, finally confirmed the restoration of the Egypt-Red Sea highway, and the key position of Egypt upon it.

In Arab Asia, off the main road, the development of communication was slower and later. It was due mainly to French companies, which built a few roads in central Syria and, between 1892 and 1911, built some five hundred miles of railway in Syria and Palestine, linking some of the main towns. The Turks themselves contributed the Ḥijāz railway, on the pilgrim route from Damascus to Medina, while the famous German-built Baghdad railway via Aleppo and Mosul was, by 1914, almost complete. Ports, bridges, canals, telegraphs and other services developed along parallel lines, while from the eighteen sixties European firms began to install water, gas, municipal transport and other amenities in some of the chief ports and other cities.

But all this vast development was concerned essentially with transit, with only limited effects on the economies of the countries traversed. The transfer of the main overland link from the Egyptian railways to the Suez Canal in 1869 for a while further diminished the direct effect on Egyptian economy. Consequently, less progress was made in the development of capital resources in the Arab lands. The most important was the extension of cotton and sugar cultivation in Egypt, thanks to the very rapid progress of irrigation with new modern equipment and to the new railways, roads and ports, giving quicker access to vaster markets.

The changes of the twentieth century were far more radical. The advent of the internal combustion engine added the aeroplane, the motor-car and the lorry to the means of locomotion. The first had revolutionised the transit routes both in their economic and their strategic aspects, while the car and the lorry have covered the whole of the Middle East with a network of new internal communications, making possible the rapid exchange of men, goods and ideas on a hitherto undreamt-of scale. The replacement of horse, ass and camel by car, bus and lorry is, more than any other single factor, changing the whole face of the Arab world. A parallel development was the exploitation of oil, by now the most important natural resource of the Middle East for the outside world. After some years' work in Persia and Anatolia, the oil companies were just extending their activities to Iraq when war broke out in 1914. The full development of Iraqi oil resources was delayed until after the peace, when a number of companies, with British interests at first predominating, began work in different parts of the country. Still more recent is the exploitation of the oil resources of Sa'ūdī Arabia, where American interests are paramount. The oil companies, with their great installations and large-scale employment of Arab labour, their pipelines and refineries, are again changing beyond recognition both the economic and the strategic picture. In Egypt the progress of industrialisation, still in its early stages, has nevertheless begun far-reaching processes of social change.

European cultural penetration was at first mainly religious, and came through the Christian minorities. The Vatican maintained contacts with Lebanese Maronite Catholics from the sixteenth century. Italian and French Capuchins and Jesuits operated in Syria, Maronite priests came to Rome and Paris. The Ottoman Sultans for long banned printing in Arabic or Turkish. The first printing-presses in the Near East were Hebrew, Greek and Syriac, used by the local Jews and Christians. But Arabic books were printed in Italy and elsewhere in the West and circulated in the Near East. The Turks began printing in Constantinople in 1729. Napoleon brought an Arabic press with him to Cairo, to print newspapers and proclamations in Arabic and Turkish. The first Muslim printing-press in the Arab world was that of Muḥammad 'Alī in Egypt. Between 1822, when it was established, and 1842 it printed 243 books, most of them textbooks for Muḥammad 'Alī's new schools and training colleges. It is significant that Turkish books outnumber Arabic books, and that works on military and naval subjects, as well as on mathematics and mechanics, are almost all in Turkish.

The religious rivalry of the great Powers for the profitable protection of holy places and Christian minorities was intensified in the nineteenth century. The most active of the missionaries in the Arab world were the French Jesuits and the American Protestant Mission, who maintained schools and colleges in Syria. They established Arabic printing-presses and printed many books, restoring to the Arabs their half-forgotten classics and translating for them some of the sources of Western knowledge. They trained a new generation of Arabs, at once more conscious of their Arab heritage and more affected by European influences.

The social effects of all these changes were more limited than one would expect. The new native middle class of traders and intellectuals came largely from the minorities and, because of its insecurity of status and separation from the population as a whole, it was unable to play its full role. But this new class spoke and wrote in Arabic. Mission-educated Syrian Christians established newspapers and periodicals in Egypt as well as Syria, and reached a wider public as more and more of the population were affected by economic and social change. It was in this period that Arab nationalism was born. It was of mingled origin. To the old Arab dislike of Turks and the urgent mistrust of the encroaching and alien West were added the European idea of nationality and a revival of the Arabic language and culture. Nationalism was strongest among the Christians, least affected by the Muslim ideal of unity, most by economic change and Western cultural influence. The Christian could not subscribe to the pan-Islamic idea which was the modern political expression of the old community of Islam. He sought instead to give a new expression, in national rather than religious terms, to the solidarity and resentments of the East against the invading West. For Muslims the two forms of expression were never really distinguished. The basic sentiment of identity was religious and social, the complete society of Islam expressed sometimes in national terms, sometimes in religious terms as synonymous and interchangeable sets of words denoting the same basic reality.

The advance of a nationalist movement was accelerated by the coming of direct European control, at first on the periphery of the Arab world—the French in Algeria, 1830, the British in Aden, 1839—then in its very heart. In 1882, the British occupied Egypt, in the very centre of the Arab world. The occupation led to an intensive development of the nationalist movement in Egypt, this time more local because with infinitely more concrete grievances and objectives.

By this time the nationalist movement was politically expressed—in political societies and then in parties. This marks another important change. The old religious forms of social expression were not dead. In Arabia the Wahhābī movement burst into life again at the beginning of the twentieth century, when ‘Abd al-‘Azīz ibn Su‘ūd began a process of expansion in the course of which the devoted Wahhābī warriors added most of Arabia to his Najdī patrimony. He annexed Ḥasā in 1913, Jabal Shammar in 1921, the Ḥijāz in 1924–5, and in 1932 proclaimed the new kingdom of Sa'ūdī Arabia with Wahhābism as its official creed. But the main organised expression was in most Arab countries political in the Western manner—until, after the Second World War, the sudden rise of militant religious brotherhoods seemed to indicate a return to an older pattern of loyalty and association.

This Westernisation of public life was to a large extent external. The real basis of society had not yet fundamentally changed. The legal abolition of feudal rights left the effective feudal relationship of landlord and peasant but little altered, with the former still enjoying a monopoly of effective leadership. The trading classes were non-Muslim—mainly outside the struggle. The ruling class was still the same, still with the same basic ideas and interests. The west European political apparatus of parliaments and elections, parties and programmes, newspapers and appeals to "public opinion" as the source of authority was borrowed ready-made and superimposed on a foundation of social reality to which it did not yet correspond. Hence the strong religious character of such movements as went beyond small cliques. Even the young Turk revolution of 1908 had only limited effects among the Arabs still under Ottoman rule. The replacement of Islam by Turkism as the basis of the Ottoman Empire and the programme of Turkification produced some reaction in Syria, hardly any in Iraq or Arabia.

The war of 1914 found Muslim feeling still predominant. Most Muslim Arabs were still for the Turks, who found sympathy also in British-occupied Egypt. But the pressures of the war years and the activities of the Allies led to a rapid development of Arab nationalism. In 1916 the British succeeded in organising an Arab revolt in the Ḥijāz, and in return for immediate material aid and the promise of Arab independence after the war, Bedouin auxiliaries aided the British forces in the conquest of Syria.

The peace settlement fell far short of the full hopes of the Arabs, but nevertheless gave them much. New states were set up in Iraq, Syria, Lebanon, Transjordan and Palestine, where

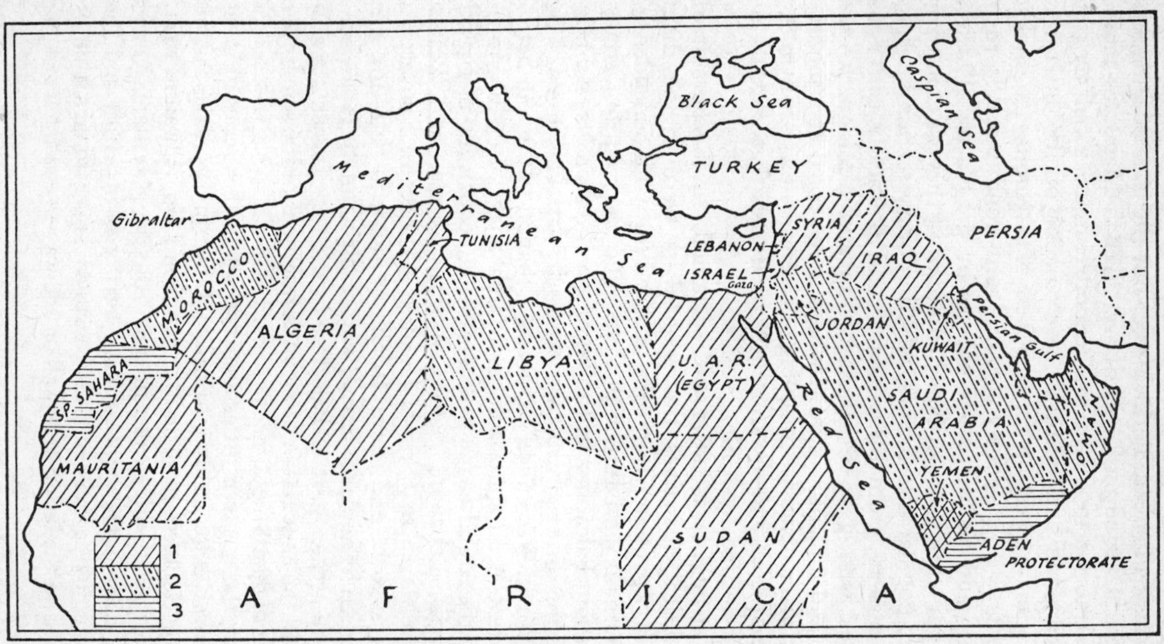

Key to the Arab world today (May 1966)
1 Republics; 2 Monarchies; 3 Dependencies

Allied arms had ended Turkish rule. But the coveted independence was deferred and British and French Mandates established. Arab disappointment, rendered more vocal by the rapid economic and cultural development of the inter-war years, found expression in a series of vigorous nationalist movements, still religiously coloured, still conditioned in their leadership and many of their policies by the old social order. But in spite of this, or perhaps because of it, they were in their time true popular movements, affecting every section of Arab Muslim society, from the educated and politically conscious minorities who gave their leadership and ideology, to the illiterate and unhappy peasant whom they served as a mouthpiece for his inarticulate mingling of resentment and fear in the presence of alien and incomprehensible forces that were dislocating his entire way of life.

The struggle was bitter and sustained. In the pursuit of their political objectives the nationalists were in the main successful. Egypt and Iraq soon attained formal independence, and the main anti-Imperialist struggle centred on Syria-Lebanon and Palestine. In the latter the situation was complicated by the development of the Jewish National Home. The Second World War added Syria and Lebanon to the number of independent Arab states and in March 1945, after long preparation, the Arab League was constituted, consisting of Egypt, Iraq, Syria, Lebanon, Sa'ūdī Arabia, Yemen and Transjordan. In March 1946, the last-named also became a sovereign state. In 1948 the end of the British Mandate in Palestine was accompanied by an Arab-Jewish war, resulting in the incorporation of the greater part of Palestine in the new Jewish state of Israel, and the annexation of all but a fragment of the remainder to the Jordanian kingdom.

During the nineteen fifties and sixties a further series of independent Arab states came into being: Libya in 1951, the Sudan, Tunisia and Morocco in 1956, Mauritania in 1960, Kuwait in 1961, Algeria in 1962, South Yemen in 1967. All save Mauritania joined the Arab League. Only the Spanish territories in Africa and the Sheikhdoms in the Persian Gulf remained under foreign rule or influence—and the latter were well on the way to independence.

The Second World War brought other changes. Although the Arab states took no effective part in it, they were profoundly affected. Allied and Axis propagandists wooed them by every means at their disposal; Allied and Axis armies lived and fought on their soil, employing thousands of Arabs in supply, maintenance and other services, enriching some and dislocating the lives of others. The economic and social stresses due to war conditions forced an increasing proportion of the population to consider the problems of their public life in terms which had not hitherto occurred to them. The economic change due to industrialisation and war and the intellectual effects of the spread of education brought the emergence of new interests, new ideas and new leaders, dissatisfied with purely political liberation, which many of them felt to be a sham, challenging the still unbroken domination of the old rulers and leaders. The influence of Nazi Germany, once so dangerous, ended with her military defeat; but a new alignment of great power rivalries again filled the East with the clash of conflicting interests and ideologies, bringing new and tempting opportunities for short-term political success, distracting attention from the real problems of a society in transition.

Once again, as in the days when the advance of the Arab warriors brought their faith into contact with Hellenism and engendered a new and fruitful offspring, Islam today stands face to face with an alien civilisation that challenges many of its fundamental values and appeals seductively to many of its followers. This time, the forces of resistance are far stronger. Islam is no longer a new faith, hot and malleable from the Arabian crucible, but an old and institutionalised religion, set by centuries of usage and tradition into rigid patterns of conduct and belief. But if the metal is harder, so too is the hammer—for the challenge of today is incomparably more radical, more aggressive, more pervasive—and it comes not from a conquered, but a conquering world. The impact of the West, with its railways and printing-presses, aeroplanes and cinemas, factories and universities, oil-prospectors and archaeologists, machine-guns and ideas, has shattered beyond repair the traditional structure of economic life, affecting every Arab in his livelihood and his leisure, his private and public life, demanding a readjustment of the inherited social, political and cultural forms.

In these problems of readjustment the Arab peoples have a choice of several paths; they may submit to one or other of the contending versions of modern civilisation that are offered to them, merging their own culture and identity in a larger and dominating whole; or they may try to turn their backs upon the West and all its works, pursuing the mirage of a return to the lost theocratic ideal, arriving instead at a refurbished despotism that has borrowed from the West its machinery both of exploitation and repression and its verbiage of intolerance, or finally—and for this the removal of the irritant of foreign interference is a prerequisite—they may succeed in renewing their society from within, meeting the West on terms of equal co-operation, absorbing something of both its science and humanism, not only in shadow but in substance, in a harmonious balance with their own inherited tradition.

CHRONOLOGICAL TABLE

B.C.

853. First mention of Arabs, in an inscription of Shalmaneser III.

65. Pompey visits Petra—first Roman contact with the Nabatean kingdom.

25–24. Expedition of Aelius Gallus to southern Arabia.

A.D.

105–6. Fall of the Nabatean kingdom, part of which becomes a Roman province.

ca. 250. Rise of "Kingdom" of Palmyra.

273. Aurelian suppresses Palmyra.

525. Fall of Ḥimyar—the Ethiopians occupy southern Arabia.

575. Persian occupation of southern Arabia, which for a few years becomes a satrapy.

602. End of Arab principality of Ḥīra, on Iraq–Arabian borderlands.

622. Hijra of Muḥammad from Mecca to Medina—beginning of Islamic era.

630. Muḥammad conquers Mecca.

632. Death of Muḥammad. Abū Bakr becomes the first Caliph.

633–37. Arabs conquer Syria and Iraq.

639–42. Conquest of Egypt.

656. Murder of 'Uthmān—beginning of first civil war in Islam.

657–59. Battle of Siffīn.

661. Murder of 'Alī—beginning of Umayyad dynasty.

680. Massacre of Ḥusain and 'Alids at Karbalā.

683–90. Second civil war.

685–87. Revolt of Mukhtār in Iraq—beginning of extremist Shī'a.

696. 'Abd al-Malik introduces Arab coinage, as part of reorganisation of imperial administration.

710. Muslims land in Spain.

A.D.

750. Fall of Umayyads, accession of 'Abbāsids.
751. Arabs capture Chinese paper-makers in Central Asia; use of paper begins to spread westward across Islamic Empire.
756. Umayyad prince 'Abd ar-Raḥmān becomes independent Amīr of Cordova.
762–63. Foundation of Baghdad by Manṣūr.
788–. Independent Idrīsid dynasty in Morocco.
799–800. Independent Aghlabid dynasty in Tunisia.
803. Hārūn ar-Rashīd deposes Barmecides.
809–13. Civil war of Amīn and Ma'mūn.
813–33. Reign of Ma'mūn—development of Arabic science and letters.
825–. Aghlabids of Tunisia begin conquest of Sicily.
833–42. Reign of Mu'taṣim—beginning of Turkish domination.
836. Foundation of Sāmarrā.
868–. Aḥmad b. Ṭūlūn, a Turkish general, founds a dynasty in Egypt and later Syria.
869–83. Revolt of negro slaves in southern Iraq.
871–. Rise of Ṣaffārids in Persia.
877. Death of Ḥunain b. Iṣḥāq, translator of Greek scientific works into Arabic.
890. First appearance of Carmathians in Iraq.
901–06. Carmathian bands active in Syria, Palestine, Mesopotamia.
910. Establishment of Fāṭimid Caliphate in North Africa.
925. Death of physician Rāzī (Rhases).
929. 'Abd ar-Raḥmān III of Cordova adopts title of Caliph.
932. Persian Buwaihid dynasty established in West Persia.
935. Creation of office of *Amīr al-Umarā*, commander in chief of Turkish guards in the capital, and effective ruler.
945. Buwaihids occupy Baghdad.
969. Fāṭimids conquer Egypt—found Cairo.
ca 970. Seljuq Turks enter territories of Caliphate from East.
1030. Umayyad Caliphate of Spain breaks up into "Party Kingdoms".

A.D.

1037. Death of Ibn Sīnā (Avicenna).
1048. Death of Bīrūnī.
1055. Seljuqs take Baghdad.
1056–57. Hilālī Arab invaders sack Qairawān.
1061. Normans take Messina—begin conquest of Sicily.
1070–80. Seljuqs occupy Syria and Palestine.
1085. Christians capture Toledo.
1086. Almoravid victory at Sagrajas.
1090. Ḥasan-i Ṣabbāḥ seizes Alamūt.
1094. Death of Fāṭimid Caliph Mustanṣir—split in Ismā'īlī movement—Ḥasan-i Ṣabbāḥ leads extremist (Assassin) wing.
1096. Crusaders arrive in Near East.
1099. Crusaders take Jerusalem.
1111. Death of Ghazālī.
1127. Zangī, a Seljuq officer, seizes Mosul—begins Muslim reaction against Crusaders.
1171. Saladin declares Fāṭimid Caliphate at an end—founds Ayyūbid dynasty in Syria and Egypt.
1187. Battle of Ḥaṭṭīn. Saladin defeats Crusaders and captures Jerusalem.
1220. Mongols conquer eastern territories of the Caliphate.
1236. Christians capture Cordova.
1250–60. Emergence of Mamlūk Sultanate in Egypt and Syria, from the decay of the Ayyūbid kingdoms.
1254. Alphonso X establishes a school of Latin and Arabic studies in Seville.
1258. Mongols under Hülekü Khān capture Baghdad and end the Caliphate.
1260. Mamlūks defeat Mongols at 'Ain Jālūt in Palestine.
1348. Construction of the Gate of Justice at the Alhambra, Granada.
1400–01. Tīmūr ravages Syria.
1406. Death of Ibn Khaldūn.
1492. Christians capture Granada.
1498. Vasco da Gama sails to India via Cape of Good Hope.

A.D.

1517. Ottomans conquer Syria and Egypt—destroy Mamlūk Sultanate.

1535. First Capitulations granted by Ottoman Sultan to France.

1639. Ottomans finally wrest Iraq from Persia.

1792. Death of Muḥammad ibn 'Abd al-Wahhāb, founder of Wahhābī sect in Arabia.

1798–1801. French occupation of Egypt.

1805–. Muḥammad 'Alī becomes effective ruler of Egypt.

1809. Beginning of regular shipping service from India to Suez.

1820. British pact with Arab Sheikhs on the Persian Gulf coast—beginning of British supremacy in the area.

1822. Muḥammad 'Alī establishes printing-press in Egypt.

1830. French invade Algeria.

1831–40. Egyptian occupation of Syria.

1836. British steamboat service established on Iraqi inland waterways.

1836. Beginning of regular British steamship service to Egypt and Syria.

1839. British occupation of Aden.

1851–57. Alexandria–Cairo–Suez Railway built.

1861. Creation of autonomous Lebanon.

1869. Suez Canal opened.

1881. French occupy Tunisia.

1882. British occupy Egypt.

1901–. Ibn Sa'ūd begins the restoration of the Sa'ūdī amirate of Najd.

1908. Young Turk Revolution.

1911–12. Italians seize Libya.

1916. Arab revolt in Ḥijāz. Sharīf Ḥusain assumes title of King.

1918. End of Ottoman rule in Arab lands.

1920. Mandates established for Syria and Lebanon (French), Palestine, Transjordan and Iraq (British).

1924–25. Ibn Sa'ūd conquers Ḥijāz.

1932. End of Mandate in Iraq.

1932. Ibn Sa'ūd proclaims Sa'ūdī Arabian Kingdom.

A.D.

1934. Ibn Sa'ūd defeats the Yemen in short war. Peace treaty of Ṭā'if.

1936. Anglo-Egyptian treaty, recognising independence of Egypt.

1941. End of Mandate for Syria and Lebanon, which become independent republics.

1945. League of Arab States formed.

1946. Britain recognises independence of Transjordan, which becomes a monarchy.

1948. End of Mandate for Palestine—establishment of state of Israel—Arab-Jewish war.

1951. Libya becomes an independent kingdom.

1953. Egypt becomes a republic.

1953. Ibn Sa'ūd dies.

1954. Colonel Jamāl 'Abd al-Nāṣir becomes leader in Egypt.

1955. British evacuation of Suez Canal zone—signature of Baghdad Pact.

1956. Sudan, Tunisia and Morocco become independent—Egypt nationalises Suez Canal—Israeli campaign in Sinai—Anglo-French expedition to Suez.

1957. Tunisia becomes a republic.

1958. Formation of United Arabic Republic—Iraq becomes a republic.

1960. Mauritania becomes independent.

1961. Kuwait becomes independent—Syria withdraws from the United Arab Republic—"Arab socialism" adopted in Egypt.

1962. Algeria becomes independent—Republican revolution in the Yemen.

1963. Revolutions in Syria and Iraq.

1965. Revolution in Algeria.

1967. Israel-Arab war.
South Yemen becomes independent.

OUTLINE BIBLIOGRAPHY

Detailed and annotated bibliographies will be found in Jean Sauvaget's *Introduction to the History of the Muslim East: a bibliographical guide*, based on the second edition as recast by Claude Cahen (English translation: Berkeley and Los Angeles, 1965); Spuler, B., and Forrer, L. *Der Vordere Orient in islamischer Zeit.* (Berne, 1954), and Pearson, J. D. *Index Islamicus 1906–1955* and *Index Islamicus Supplement 1956–1960* (Cambridge, 1959 and 1962.)

GENERAL INTRODUCTORY WORKS:

Gibb, H. A. R. *The Arabs.* (Oxford, 1940.) (In "Oxford Pamphlets on World Affairs.")

Planhol, X. de. *The World of Islam.* (English translation, Cornell, 1959.)

Brockelmann, C. *History of the Islamic Peoples.* (English translation, London, 1949.)

Hitti, P. K. *History of the Arabs.* (London, 1946.)

Bart'old, V. V. *Mussulman Culture.* (English translation, Calcutta, 1934.)

Gabrieli, F. *The Arabs, a compact history.* (English translation, New York, 1963.)

Saunders, J. J. *A History of Medieval Islam.* (London, 1965.)

Sourdel, D. *Islam.* (English translation, New York, 1962.)

Spuler, B. *Geschichte der islamischen Länder.* 2 parts. (Leiden, 1952–53.)

Hottinger, A. *The Arabs; their History, Culture and Place in the Modern World.* (English translation, London, 1963.)

Cambridge Mediaeval History. Vol. II, chapters 10, 11, 12; Vol. IV, chapters on Islam.

COLLECTIONS OF STUDIES:

Becker, C. H. *Islamstudien.* 2 vols. (Berlin, 1924.)

Goldziher, I. *Muhammedanische Studien.* 2 vols. (Halle, 1890.)

COLLECTIONS OF STUDIES (*cont.*):

Nallino, C. A. *Raccolta di Scritti*. Vol. III. (Rome, 1941.)

Gibb, H. A. R. *Studies on the Civilization of Islam*. (London, 1962.)

Brunschvig, R., and Schacht, J. *Studia Islamica*. (Paris, 1953—.)

C. Snouck Hurgronje. *Selected Works*. Edited in English and in French by G-H. Bousquet and J. Schacht. (Leiden, 1957.)

Lewis, B., and Holt, P. M. (editors). *Historians of the Middle East*. (London, 1962.)

REGIONAL HISTORIES:

Egypt:

Lane-Poole, S. *History of Egypt in the Middle Ages*. (London, 1925.)

Hanotaux, G. (editor). *Histoire de la Nation Egyptienne*. Vols. IV and V. (Paris, 1926.)

Précis de l'Histoire de l'Egypte. Vol. II, Munier and Wiet: *l'Egypte Byzantine et Musulmane*. Vol. III, Combe, Bainville and Driault: *l'Egypte Ottomane*, etc. (Cairo, 1933.)

Syria–Lebanon:

Lammens, H. *La Syrie. Précis Historique*. 2 vols. (Beirut, 1921.)

Hitti, P. K. *History of Syria*. (London, 1951.); *Lebanon in History*. (London, 1957.)

Chebli, M. *Une Histoire du Liban à l'époque des émirs (1635–1841)*. (Beirut, 1955.)

Ismail, A. *Histoire du Liban du XVIIe siècle à nos jours*. Vol. I. (Paris, 1955.) Vol. IV. (Beirut, 1958.)

Iraq:

Longrigg, S. H. *Four Centuries of Modern Iraq*. (Oxford, 1925.)

North Africa:

Marçais, G. *La Berbérie Musulmane et l'Orient au Moyen Age*. (Paris, 1946.)

Julien, C. A. *Histoire de l'Afrique du Nord*. Vol. II, *De la conquête arabe à 1830*. 2nd revised edition. (Paris, 1952.)

WORKS OF REFERENCE:

Caetani, L. *Chronographia Islamica*. 5 vols. (Paris, 1912.)

Lane-Poole, S. *The Mohammedan Dynasties*, Chronological and Genealogical Tables. (London, 1894.)

Encyclopaedia of Islam. 4 vols. and supplement. (Leiden, 1913–38.)

Encyclopaedia of Islam. New edition. (Leiden, 1954 ff.—in course of publication.)

Hazard, H. W. *Atlas of Islamic History*. (Princeton, 1952.)

Historical Atlas of the Muslim Peoples. Compiled by R. Roolvink and others. (Amsterdam, 1957.)

Pareja, F. M., and others. *Islamología*. 2 vols. (Madrid, 1952–54.)

CHAPTERS I AND II:

Levi Della Vida, G. Pre-Islamic Arabia, in Faris, N.A. *The Arab Heritage*. (Princeton, 1944.)

Muir, Sir W. *The Life of Muhammad*. (Edinburgh, 1923.)

Tor Andrae. *Muhammad, his Life and his Faith*. (English translation, London, 1936.)

Buhl, F. *Das Leben Muhammads*. (German translation, Leipzig, 1930.)

Caetani, L. *Studi di Storia Orientale*. Vols. I and III. (Milan, 1911–14.)

Guidi, M. *Storia e Cultura degli Arabi fino alla Morte di Maometto*. (Florence, 1951.)

Watt, W. M. *Muhammad at Mecca*. (Oxford, 1953.)

Watt, W. M. *Muhammad at Medina*. (Oxford, 1956.)

Blachère, R. *Le Problême de Mahomet*. (Paris, 1952.)

Gaudefroy-Demombynes, M. *Mahomet*. (Paris, 1957.)

Guillaume, A. *The Life of Muhammad*. (Oxford, 1954.)

Paret, R. *Mohammed und der Koran*. (Stuttgart, 1957.)

Jeffery, A. (ed). *Islam: Muhammad and his religion*. (New York, 1958.)

Rodinson, M. *Mahomet*. (Paris, 1961.)

CHAPTERS III–VI:

Muir, Sir W. *The Caliphate, its Rise, Decline and Fall*. (Edinburgh, 1924.)

CHAPTER III–VI (*cont.*):

Gaudefroye-Demombynes and Platonov. *Le Monde Musulman et Byzantin jusqu'aux Croisades.* (Paris, 1931.)

Diehl, C., and Marçais, G. *Le Monde Oriental de 395 à 1081.* (Paris, 1936.)

Wellhausen, J. *The Arab Kingdom and its Fall.* (English translation, Calcutta, 1927.)

Nöldeke, T. *Sketches from Eastern History.* (English translation, Edinburgh, 1892.)

Von Kremer, A. *Culturgeschichte des Orients unter den Chalifen.* 2 vols. (Vienna, 1875.) Partially translated by S. Khuda Bukhsh in *The Orient under the Caliphs* (Calcutta, 1920), and in *Studies, Indian and Islamic* (London, 1927).

Sourdel, D. *Le Vizirat 'abbaside.* 2 vols. (Damascus, 1959–60.)

Bowen, H. *Life and Times of 'Ali ibn 'Isa* (Cambridge, 1928.)

Mez, A. *The Renaissance of Islam* (English translation, London, 1937.)

Bosworth, C. E. *The Ghaznavids.* (Edinburgh, 1963.)

Kabir, M. *The Buwayhid Dynasty of Baghdad.* (Calcutta, 1964.)

Laoust, H. *Les Schismes dans l'Islam.* (Paris, 1965.)

Sadighi, G. H. *Les Mouvements Religieux Iraniens.* (Paris, 1938.)

Lewis, B. *The Origins of Ismā'īlism.* (Cambridge, 1940.)

Ivanow, W. *The Alleged Founder of Ismailism.* (Bombay, 1946.)

Tritton, A. S. *The Caliphs and their non-Muslim Subjects.* (Oxford, 1930.)

Goitein, S. D. *Jews and Arabs.* (New York, 1955.)

CHAPTER VII:

Lévi-Provençal, E. *La Civilisation Arabe en Espagne* (Second edition, Paris, 1948); *L'Espagne musulmane au Xe siècle* (Paris, 1932); *Histoire de l'Espagne musulmane.* 3 vols. (Second edition, Paris, 1950–53).

Dozy, R. *Histoire des Musulmans d'Espagne.* 3 vols. (Revised edition, Leiden, 1932.)

Gonzalez Palencia, A. *Historia de la España musulmana.* (Barcelona, 1932.)

CHAPTER VII (*cont.*):

Watt, W. M. *A History of Islamic Spain.* (Edinburgh, 1965.)

Sanchez-Albornoz, C. España y el Islam. (*Revista de Occidente*, LXX, Madrid, 1929.)

Amari, M. *Storia dei Musulmani di Sicilia.* 5 vols. (Revised edition, Catania, 1933–39.)

CHAPTER VIII:

Levy, R. *The Social Structure of Islam.* (Cambridge, 1957.)

Von Grunebaum, G. E. *Medieval Islam.* (Second edition, Chicago, 1953.)

Von Grunebaum, G. E. *Islam, Essays in the Nature and Growth of a Cultural Tradition.* (The American Anthropological Association, 1955.)

Gibb, H. A. R. *Arabic Literature, an Introduction.* (Second edition, Oxford, 1963.)

Nicholson, R. A. *Literary History of the Arabs.* (Cambridge, 1930.)

Gabrieli, F. *Storia della Letteratura araba.* (Milan, 1951.)

Mieli, A. *La Science Arabe.* (Leiden, 1938.)

Browne, E. G. *Arabian Medicine.* (Cambridge, 1921.)

De Boer, T. J. *The History of Philosophy in Islam.* (English translation, London, 1933.)

Goldziher, I. *Vorlesungen über den Islam.* (Heidelberg, 1910.) (French translation by F. Arin, *Le Dogme et la Loi de l'Islam*, Paris, 1920.)

Gibb, H. A. R. *Mohammedanism.* (Second edition, Oxford, 1953.)

Arberry, A. J. *Sufism.* (London, 1950.)

Macdonald, D. B. *Muslim Theology, Jurisprudence and Constitutional Theory.* (New York, 1903.)

Schacht, J. *An Introduction to Islamic Law.* (Oxford, 1964.)

Coulson, N. J. *A History of Islamic Law.* (Edinburgh, 1964.)

Khadduri, M. *War and Peace in the Law of Islam.* (Baltimore, 1955.)

Arnold, T. W. *The Caliphate.* (Oxford, 1924.)

Tyan, E. *Institutions du droit public musulman.* 2 vols. (Paris, 1954–57.)

Gardet, L. *La Cité musulmane.* (Paris, 1954.)

CHAPTER VIII (*cont.*):

Rosenthal, E. I. J. *Political Thought in Medieval Islam.* Cambridge, 1958.)

Marçais, G. *L'Art de l'Islam.* (Paris, 1946.)

Creswell, K. A. C. *Early Muslim Architecture.* (London, 1958.)

Arnold, T. W. and Guillaume, A. *The Legacy of Islam.* (Oxford, 1931.)

CHAPTER IX:

Hodgson, M. G. S. *The Order of Assassins.* (The Hague, 1955.)

Setton, K. M. (editor-in-chief) *A History of the Crusades.* Vols. 1 and 2. (Philadelphia, 1955 and 1962.)

Stevenson, W. B. *The Crusaders in the East.* (Cambridge, 1907.)

Runciman, S. *A History of the Crusades.* 3 vols. (Cambridge, 1951–54.)

Cahen, C. *La Syrie du Nord à l'Époque des Croisades.* (Paris, 1940.)

Heyd, W. *Histoire du commerce du Levant au moyen age.* 2 vols. (Leipzig, 1885.)

Atiya, A. S. *The Crusade in the Later Middle Ages.* (London, 1938.)

Poliak, A. N. *Feudalism in Egypt, Syria, Palestine, and the Lebanon, 1250–1900.* (London, 1939.)

Brunschvig, R., and von Grunebaum, G. E. (editors): *Classicisme et Déclin culturel dans l'histoire de l'Islam.* (Paris, 1957.)

CHAPTER X:

Von Hammer, J. *Geschichte des Osmanischen Reiches.* 10 vols. Pest. 1827–35. (French translation. 18 vols. Paris, 1835–43.)

Gibb, H. A. R., and Bowen, H. *Islamic Society and the West.* I: *Islamic Society in the Eighteenth Century.* 2 parts. (Oxford, 1950–57.)

Lewis, B. *The Middle East and the West.* (London, 1964.)

Hurewitz, J. C. *Diplomacy in the Near and Middle East (1535–1956).* 2 vols. (Princeton, 1956.)

CHAPTER X (*cont.*):

Rossi, E. *Documenti sulla origine e gli sviluppi della questione araba (1875–1944)*. (Rome, 1944.)

Kirk, G. E. *A Short History of the Middle East*. 3rd edition. (London, 1955.)

Masson, P. *Histoire du commerce français dans le Levant au XVIIe siècle* (Paris, 1896); *Histoire du commerce français dans le Levant au XVIIIe siècle* (Paris, 1911.)

Wood, A. C. *A History of the Levant Company*. (London, 1935.)

Gabrieli, F. *The Arab Revival*. (English translation, London, 1961.)

Dodwell, H. H. *The Founder of Modern Egypt, a Study of Muhammad Ali*. (Cambridge, 1931.)

Hasenclever, I. *Geschichte Aegyptens im 19 Jahrhundert*. (Halle, 1917.)

Rifaat Bey, M. *The Awakening of Modern Egypt*. (London, 1947.)

Landau, J. M. *Parliaments and Parties in Egypt*. (New York, 1954.)

Safran, N. *Egypt in search of political community: an analysis of the intellectual and political evolution of Egypt, 1804–1951*. (Cambridge Mass, 1961.)

Baer, G. *The History of Landownership in modern Egypt, 1800–1950*. (London, 1962.)

Temperley, H. W. V. *England and the Near East. The Crimea*. (London, 1936.)

Toynbee, A. J. *The Islamic World since the Peace Settlement*. (Survey of International Affairs, 1925, I. Oxford, 1927), and later volumes for 1928, 30, 34, 36, 37, etc.

Gibb, H. A. R. *Whither Islam*. (London, 1932.) *Modern Trends in Islam*. (Chicago, 1947.)

Smith, W. C. *Islam in Modern History*. (Oxford, 1957.)

Laqueur, W. Z. *Communism and Nationalism in the Middle East*. (London, 1956.)

Hourani, A. *Arabic Thought in the Liberal Age*. (London, 1962.)

Haim, Sylvia G. *Arab Nationalism, an Anthology*. (Berkeley and Los Angeles, 1962.)

CHAPTER X (*cont.*):

Von Grunebaum, G. E. *Modern Islam: the search for cultural identity*. (Berkeley and Los Angeles, 1962.)

Braune, W. *Der islamische Orient zwischen Vergangenheit und Zukunft*. (Berne, 1960.)

Berque, J. *The Arabs: their History and Future*. (English translation: London, 1964.)

Berger, M. *The Arab World Today*. (London, 1962.)

Antonius, G. *The Arab Awakening*. (London, 1939.)

Kedourie, E. *England and the Middle East*. (London, 1956.)

Zeine, Z. N. *Arab-Turkish Relations and the Emergence of Arab Nationalism*. (Beirut, 1958.)

Zeine, Z. N. *The Struggle for Arab Independence*. (Beirut, 1960.)

Bullard, Sir Reader. *Britain and the Middle East*. (Second edition, London, 1952.)

Rondot, P. *The Changing Patterns of the Middle East*. (English translation, London, 1961.)

Crouchley, A. E. *The Economic Development of Modern Egypt*. (London, 1938.)

Young, G. *Egypt*. (London, 1927.)

Zayid, M. Y. *Egypt's Struggle for Independence*. (Beirut, 1965.)

Colombe, M. *l'Évolution de l'Egypte 1924–1950*. (Paris, 1951.)

Issawi, C. *Egypt in Revolution*. (London, 1963.)

Vatikiotis, P. J. *The Egyptian Army in Politics*. (Bloomington, Ind., 1961.)

Holt, P. M. *A Modern History of the Sudan*. (Second edition, London, 1963.)

Philby, H. St. J. *Saudi Arabia*. (London, 1955.)

Kelly, J. B. *Eastern Arabian Frontiers*. (London, 1964.)

Hourani, A. K. *Syria and Lebanon*. (London, 1946.)

Longrigg, S. H. *Syria and Lebanon under French Mandvte*. (London 1958.)

Salibi, K. S. *The Modern History of Lebanon*. (London 1965.)

Longrigg, S. *Iraq 1900–1950*. (London, 1953.)

Khadduri, M. *Independent Iraq: a study of Iraqi politics from 1932 to 1958*. (Second edition, London, 1960.)

Le Tourneau, R. *Évolution politique de l'Afrique du Nord musulmane 1920–1961*. (Paris, 1962.)

Khadduri, M. *Modern Libya: a study in political development*. (Baltimore, 1963.)

INDEX